in search of the

Celtic Saints

The cover shows St Kevin and the blackbird, from British Library MS Royal 13 B VIII (English, late twelfth or early thirteenth century), an anthology of texts on topography, history and marvels of the world.

www.bl.uk

Also from the Langley Press:

A Little Book of English Saints
In Search of the Northern Saints
The Voyage of St Brendan
Nicholas Breakspear: The Pope from England
The Legend of St Alban
Gilbert's Tale: The Life and Death of Thomas Becket
In Search of Bede
Bede's Life of St Cuthbert
The History of King Richard III
Mary Ann Cotton: Victorian Serial Killer

For free downloads and more from the Langley Press, visit our website:

http://tinyurl.com/lpdirect

in search of the

Celtic Saints

by

Simon Webb

The Langley Press, Durham, 2017

Contents

Gregory the Great, from BM Harley 3011

Introduction

Some time before he became pope in 590 A.D., Gregory the Great saw two blue-eyed, fair-skinned boys being offered for sale at Rome's slave-market. The boys must have stood out among the dark-haired, olive-skinned Italian natives, and Gregory, his curiosity piqued, asked where they came from.

He learned that they were from Britain, and that they were not Christians, but pagans. Expressing his regret that the devil should enjoy the command of such beautiful creatures, the future pope asked what race they belonged to. They are Angles, he was told, and the future pope approved of the name: the boys looked like angels indeed. When he asked what kingdom the boys came from, he was told, Deira: at this, Gregory said that the Angles should be snatched from *de ira*, meaning 'the wrath of God' in Latin. Learning that the king of Deira was called Aelle, Gregory said that the pagans of his kingdom should be taught to sing alleluias.

The story above is from *The Ecclesiastical History of the English People*, written in Latin by a Northumbrian scholar-monk, the Venerable Bede, who died in 735 A.D. For Bede it is part of the narrative of how his own race was snatched from the teeth of Satan.

The kingdom of Deira, where Gregory's angelic boys are supposed to have originated, lay between the Humber and Tees rivers on the east coast of Britain, and was roughly equivalent to the east of Yorkshire. Its king, Aelle, was probably an Angle himself, a descendant of the Germanic people who invaded the area late in the fifth century A.D. Part of the group historians now call the Anglo-Saxons, these invaders overran the territory to which they gave the name England, pushing many of the earlier Celtic inhabitants west into Wales. Although many of the British Celts at this time would have been Christians, the Anglo-Saxons were pagans. They had brought their own Germanic version of paganism with them across the sea, and the names of some of their gods are still preserved in the English names for the days of the week: Thursday is named after Thor, for instance.

The Anglo-Saxons divided England into

a number of small kingdoms, and many of the kings of these places claimed descent from the god Woden, after whom Wednesday is named.

It seems that Gregory, the future pope, was so taken with his angelic slave-boys that he became determined to bring news of Jesus to their pagan race. By this time, he had already become a monk: one of those rare monks who have founded their own monasteries. Gregory's monastery was named after St Andrew, and was based in his own large house on Rome's Caelian Hill – one of the seven famous hills of the Eternal City.

After he had met the English boys, Gregory set off on a long journey north and west, planning to cross the sea and convert the pagan Angles. But by this time he had become such a popular, admired and useful figure in Rome itself that he was called back after only four days of travelling. He was reconciled to his return by a locust, of all things, which settled on a page of the Bible he was reading. '*Ecce locusta*' he said, meaning 'look at the locust'. The Latin phrase sounded like '*loco sta*', meaning 'stay in place'.

When Gregory became pope, he did not,

however, forget the poor benighted Angles. In 596 he chose Augustine, the abbot of St Andrew's, his own monastery, to lead a mission to England. By one of those strange coincidences that can illuminate a dark corner of history, Augustine probably landed in England in the same year that Columba, the third of the saints whose lives are described below, died on the Scottish island of Iona.

At this time, Great Britain, the largest of the British Isles, had a very diverse population. In the north, as we shall see, there were the Picts, who shared what we now call Scotland with settlers from Ireland. The Anglo-Saxons had spread themselves over the greater part of the island to the south, but the Britons still held on in the west, in Wales and Cornwall.

Over thirty years before Augustine landed, Columba, an Irish saint, had sailed east from Ireland to the Scottish island of Iona, and begun bringing the gospel to the people of what we now think of as the Scottish mainland. Nearly forty years after Augustine disembarked, another saint, called Aidan, left Iona on a mission to convert some of the Anglo-Saxons of the north of England. Aidan was a contemporary of St

Paulinus, an Italian who was part of the second wave of missionaries send to England by Pope Gregory.

Many of the first English Christians were, therefore, converted by either missionaries from Rome, or others who stood in the Irish, or Celtic, tradition of Christianity.

Although a previous attempt to convert the Irish had been made, Irish Christianity began in earnest when St Patrick returned to the island as a missionary, an event which is traditionally supposed to have happened in 433 A.D. Although some accounts claim that Patrick had been made a bishop in Italy before he returned to Ireland, and had been sent to that green island by Pope Celestine I, the Celtic Christianity that arrived in Great Britain with Columba and, later, Aidan, was different enough from the Christianity of Augustine and Paulinus for the two to come into conflict in later years.

Historically speaking, the distinctive Celtic type of Christianity is now long lost. As we shall see, it was dealt a crippling blow at the Synod of Whitby in 664; and the church in Ireland was brought more firmly into the Roman fold during the twelfth century. This has not stopped some modern writers from looking back on the Celtic Christian centuries and regretting their passing. To some, this seems like a kind of Christianity that did not possess some of the elements that make Christianity off-putting to many modern people. It seems, to some modern enthusiasts, to have had a connection with nature and with its pagan heritage that was rich and attractive.

The term 'Celtic Christianity' combines the name of a religion founded in Palestine two thousand years ago, with that of an ancient culture that may first have appeared another thousand years earlier. The Celts were never a race, in the modern sense, but rather a linguistic and cultural group that spread over large areas of Europe and beyond, fought wars against the Romans, and were known to the ancient Greeks as the *Keltoi*.

Partly because the ancient Celts were not ultimately victorious against the Romans, their modern ancestors are concentrated in a few areas on the north-west fringes of Europe: mainly Brittany, Cornwall, Wales, Scotland and Ireland. The ancestral languages of these people have often been threatened with complete extinction over the centuries: evolved from ancient 'Common

Celtic', these languages are Welsh, Breton, Modern Irish, Scottish Gaelic, Cornish, and Manx (from the Isle of Man). The last two languages did in fact die out altogether, but have been revived in modern times.

The link between various peoples, such as the Gauls, mentioned by ancient writers like Julius Caesar, Livy and Polybius, and modern Celtic people, was not properly understood until the eighteenth and nineteenth centuries. In 1871 several of these historical loose ends were re-tied when delegates at an archaeological congress in Bologna were struck by the similarities between artefacts unearthed in widely-spaced digs in Switzerland, France and Italy.

As Nora Chadwick makes clear in her 1971 book *The Celts*, Celtic culture was illiterate in many places until quite a late date. This did not prevent the unlettered Celts from having a rich culture of the word, expressed in oral tradition. Some of the legends that had been transmitted orally for centuries were written down from the eighth century: much more material, including hymns, poems, prayers and charms, was collected from Gaelic-speaking Scots by the folklorist Alexander Carmichael (1832-1912). Known collectively as the *Carmina*

Gadelica, Carmichael's discoveries have contributed greatly to modern ideas about Celtic Christianity.

The exact nature of the distinctiveness of Celtic culture has been much discussed over the years: the question is complicated by the fact that their culture has been around for a very long time, has thrived in many different parts of the world, and has manifested itself in many ways. It might be tempting to try to find a connection between the British Museum's bronze Celtic horned helmet, which may be over two thousand years old, a hymn from the *Carmina Gadelica,* and Adomnan's biography of St Columba, but it is hard to see how such a connection could be made.

The questions of whether the ancient culture of the Celts, however it is to be characterised, gave their form of Christianity its distinctive flavour, and how that distinctiveness should be described, might take many volumes much longer than this one to answer. It is to be hoped, however, that the following account of some of the Celtic saints might add a little extra information to the argument.

SW, Durham, 2017

St Patrick, from BL Royal 20 D VI

1. Patrick

Walking to work on the morning of Thursday March the seventeenth 2016, I was passed by a jogger dressed as a bishop. He had the mitre, robe and crook, all in white, but made out of the shiny, flimsy material commonly used for fancy-dress costumes. He wished me the top of the morning, and jogged by with a big smile on his face. I was mystified by this, until I noticed that his robe was decorated with shamrocks. Ah, I thought, this man is celebrating St Patrick's day, and he's starting early.

Today the feast of St Patrick is marked all over the world, even by people who are not Christians, and have no connection with Ireland, the country which is most closely associated with the saint. The day is more a celebration of all things Irish than a festival for St Patrick himself: revellers tend to wear a lot of green in honour of the so-called 'Emerald Isle' and drink a particular brand of dark Irish beer.

It may seem foolish to jog on the streets between villages in the English county of Durham, dressed as St Patrick, but the Life of Patrick written by the twelfth-century Cumbrian monk Jocelyn of Furness includes a story that would seem to recommend marking March the seventeenth as enthusiastically as possible.

It seems that one Saint Kaennechus was walking through the Irish countryside when he came across a troop of demons 'passing along, armed with infernal instruments'. He asked them what they were about, and they were forced to answer truthfully, because he had invoked the name of the Holy Trinity before asking them his question. In the words of E.L. Swift's translation of the story, they said they had come 'to bear away the soul of a certain most wicked sinner, who for his sins deserved to be carried into hell'. Kaennechus bade the demons farewell, but ordered them to come and tell him the outcome of their infernal fishing-trip. Later, they reported that, despite his grievous crimes, the soul of their intended victim had escaped them because every year this sinner had 'celebrated with a great feast the festival of Saint Patrick, and had every day repeated certain chapters of the hymn which had been composed in his honour'.

St Patrick's Day is becoming increasingly popular in modern times, though it is named after a saint who probably lived over fifteen hundred years ago. Patrick seems, however, to have been destined to make a lasting impression. His wildly successful missionary journeys to Ireland were even prophesied by the pagan druids, who were in control of the religious life of the Irish people before he came.

Three druids, called Lochru, Luchat-Mael and Conn, predicted Patrick's mission some two or three years before he arrived. Their prophesies said that a great prophet would come to Ireland, who would follow a set of instructions previously unknown to the Irish, and win vast numbers of the natives to his cause. This prophet, they said, would destroy the statues of the pagan gods, and also knock kings off their thrones. He would wear a garment with a hole for his head in the middle of it, and he would build 'pointed music-houses' with conical roofs, and altars at their east ends, where the people would say 'amen, amen'. Worst news of all for the pagan prophets, their own religion would disappear, and this mysterious new religion would hold sway over Ireland, forever.

This prophecy is said to have caused an Irish king called Leogaire to take against Patrick, as soon as the saint reached his country. As we shall see, this pagan king and the Christian saint fought against each other for a long time.

The details of Patrick's life have come down to us in a number of texts, including some writings that may be from his own hand. The sources often disagree with each other, and some of the later sources have more detail than the earlier ones, suggesting that the later authors added information for which they had no real evidence. Despite its length, and the many fantastic stories it contains, the Life of Patrick by Jocelyn of Furness does not include the familiar tale of Patrick trying to explain the nature of the Holy Trinity by using a shamrock-leaf. *Patrick's Breastplate* (a beautiful hymn attributed to the saint), the tale of his banishing the snakes from Ireland, and indeed many other aspects of Patrick's life, are likewise absent from the earliest sources.

Some think that Patrick first came to Ireland as a missionary when he was in his mid-forties, but he had probably first arrived on the island some thirty years earlier, not as a missionary, but as a slave.

At the age of sixteen, Patrick was captured by Irish marauders and sold to Milchu, a local Irish king who was also a priest of the druids' religion. Despite his sudden immersion in a pagan culture, Patrick retained the religion he had been raised in, and prayed fervently to the Christian God. His first sojourn in Ireland may have strengthened his Christianity: it must also have made him familiar with the local language and culture.

It is not uncommon to read that individuals who later became saints underwent a period of hardship in their earlier years; a period that might easily have wrecked them both physically and mentally, but which actually revealed their inner strength by making them more faithful and resilient. Patrick himself even prescribed a period of extreme hardship for one Machaldus, a sort of Irish land-pirate, who had been a devotee of paganism until, by performing some miracles for him, the saint showed him the error of his ways.

In the words of Jocelyn, Patrick told Machaldus that he should 'utterly renounce his native soil and give all his substance to the poor'. The saint then:

clothed Machaldus in a vile and rough garment, and chained him with chains of iron, and cast the key thereof into the ocean. Likewise he commanded him to enter, alone, without oars, into a boat made only of hides, and that on whatsoever country he should land under the guidance of the Lord there should he serve Him even unto the end of his days.

After six years as a slave, Patrick himself managed to escape from his cruel master, and returned to his parents, Calphurnius and Concessa. This couple are supposed to have been high-ranking Christians in post-Roman Britain, living at Kilpatrick, near Dumbarton on the River Clyde, in the west of what we now call Scotland.

The twenty or more years between Patrick's escape from slavery and his return to Ireland as a missionary may have been spent training for the priesthood in France. According to some accounts, he journeyed to Britain with a French bishop called St Germain, but abandoned Great Britain when he heard the cry of the unborn children of Ireland, begging him to return. Other accounts state that Patrick had been officially ordered to go directly to Ireland by the aforementioned Pope Celestine I, who had previously made him bishop of Turin.

Patrick was not the first missionary to have been dispatched to the Emerald Isle: he was following in the footsteps of a man called Palladius, whose mission seems to have been a near-total failure. We will meet with another failed predecessor when we come to the life of St Aidan, missionary to Northumbria.

In the introduction to his 1853 English translation of what is supposed to be one of Patrick's own writings, his *Confession*, the Church of Ireland curate Thomas Olden argues that Patrick could not have had a continental training in the ways of the Roman Catholic Church, and could not have had any contact with any pope. Olden's argument is an attempt by a Protestant to detach the historical Patrick from Roman Catholicism: he suggests that the saint's background had more to do with the early Celtic British Church which, Olden suggests, was closer to the Anglicanism of the nineteenth century than medieval Roman Catholicism.

Olden's argument smacks of the anti-Catholic prejudice that was a nasty characteristic of Anglicanism for centuries, but the idea that the more Catholic aspects of

Patrick's story were later accretions certainly holds some water.

Whether or not he was a newly-minted Catholic bishop at the time, Patrick performed many miracles in Ireland. In fact, most sources re-tell his time as a missionary there not as a coherent narrative, but as a series of miraculous episodes that could have been arranged in any order by the hagiographer, or writer of saints' lives. This is a familiar phenomenon to anyone who has read a few lives of the saints written in medieval times: after an account of the saint's birth and childhood, it is miracle, miracle, miracle until we learn of the saint's death, and then the miracles he or she performed after death.

Patrick began his return-voyage to Ireland by giving a spectacular demonstration of both the power and the compassion of his God. As Patrick's ship was being prepared for the crossing, a leper appeared and started begging to be allowed to cross with him. The sailors, no doubt fearing infection, refused to let the leper on board. Nothing daunted, Patrick threw a stone altar he happened to have with him, into the sea. The leper was able to ride across to Ireland on the amazingly buoyant altar in perfect safety, and he landed at the same time as Patrick.

The altar that is central to this story may be the same one that followed after the saint, like a loyal dog, as he made his way to Connaght in the west. Nobody could make out how it continued to move, but it followed Patrick up hill and down dale until he instructed it to remain still.

Patrick's devoted altar is just one example of the personal attractiveness of the saint. Wherever he went, he acquired followers: so many, in fact, that he often had to tell them not to tag along, but to remain fixed in one place, like his wandering altar. At this time, Ireland was divided into many petty kingdoms; and even when Patrick was confronted by angry kings who resisted his preaching, he found that the kings' wives, children, soldiers, and even the druids they kept as spiritual advisers, would come over to Patrick's side and want to follow him.

One of these would-be companions of Patrick was Glarcus, a giant whom the saint raised from the dead, using his famous staff, which was supposed to have been the staff owned by Jesus himself. Because the giant looked so terrifying, the saint would not let him travel with him, though he begged to be allowed to do so. Perhaps Patrick feared that Glarcus's looks would scare off potential converts.

Looks were also a problem for one Eugenius, a wealthy, high-ranking Irishman who, however, regarded himself as an ugly, deformed dwarf. After the poor fellow had become a Christian, Patrick listened to Eugenius's complaints about his appearance, and arranged a miracle to improve his new convert's looks. First he asked Eugenius to pick out a handsome man whom he would like to resemble. Eugenius picked one Roichus, Patrick's personal librarian, who was 'beautiful in his form above all men in those countries dwelling'. The saint could not effect the transformation straight away: the two men had to sleep under the same blanket for a whole night, and in the morning they looked identical; except that only Roichus's hair was tonsured like a monk's. When Patrick had also improved Eugenius's height, his work on his new convert was done.

The giant whom Patrick reclaimed from the clutches of death a reminder of the celebrated giants of Irish folklore, such as Finn MacCool, who is supposed to have constructed the famous Giant's Causeway in

Antrim. Like several of the people whom Patrick raised from the dead, Glarcus was able to confirm, from his experience in the land of the dead, that the Christian view of the universe that the saint described in his preaching was in fact correct. As soon as he had been restored from the dust, the giant said, 'How great thanks do I give unto thee, o beloved and chosen of God! who even for one hour hast released me from unspeakable torments and from the gates of hell!'

The Christian concern with the after-life that pervades Jocelyn's version of the life of Patrick gives it an emphasis that may seem alien, even off-putting, to modern readers. Since the after-life was regarded as infinite, and one's natural life infinitely short in comparison, to Jocelyn it seemed preferable to live a short, perfect life and go straight to heaven, than to live a long, sinful life and be damned at the end of it.

The boon of a short, perfect life was granted to Ethne and Fedella, the beautiful daughters of the aforementioned King Leogaire Mac Neill. These girls had been educated by the druids at their father's court, and when they first encountered Patrick, they asked him a series of interesting questions, such as might come into the heads of people brought up to believe in a multitude of gods.

According to an eighth-century account, they asked Patrick if he and his companions were from the *sidhe*, mysterious mounds of earth where the *aes sidhe*, a species of supernatural beings, were supposed to live. They also asked Patrick if he himself was a god, and if not, who his god was? And where was this god to be found? In heaven, or on earth, or under the earth, or in the sea, or rivers, on the hills, or in the valleys? What does he look like? Is he young or old? Is he immortal? Does he have children? Is he wealthy? How can we see him?

The saint's answer showed that he had noticed the sisters' last question in particular. Soon the sisters were converted, baptised, given nuns' veils, and then allowed to fall asleep and die almost immediately. That, Patrick might have muttered to himself, is how you get to see God.

A good death could be regarded as a great gift in the universe of Jocelyn's Life of Patrick: likewise a long life could be shown to be a curse. The saint had a valuable ally in the shape of a fellow Briton called Moccheus, who had settled in Ireland 'for the sake of God'. But when Patrick and Moccheus were studying the Old Testament book of Genesis together, Patrick's friend expressed his doubts about the possibility of 'the patriarchs before the Flood' having lived for nine hundred years, as stated in that book. Patrick responded to his friend's doubts by reminding Moccheus that 'the whole canonical Scripture was written and dictated by the finger of God', and prophesied that the doubter himself would live for three hundred years. Like all of Patrick's prophecies, this proved to be accurate.

Patrick seems to have had a mental list of tasks he wanted to accomplish in Ireland: among them was the conversion of Milchu, his old master. The saint journeyed to the country around Ballymena, near the northeast tip of the island of Ireland, intending to give Milchu not only Christianity, but also the price of his own freedom – i.e., Patrick wanted to buy his freedom according to law, having previously stolen himself away from bondage. This suggests that, far from being illegal, slavery was governed by a set of formal laws, in ancient Ireland.

As he rounded the top of a nearby hill and looked down on Milchu's home, Patrick saw that his old master, terrified at the prospect of being made into a Christian, had piled up all his belongings, set them alight, and thrown himself on the fire.

With his typical saints' ability to see rather more of the universe than most of us, Patrick was able to watch Milchu's soul spinning down into the torments of hell. He also saw that his old master's royal dynasty had been broken by his fiery suicide, and that in future none of his descendants would be kings.

Another king who tried to escape Patrick's influence was a man called Victor. One night, hearing of the saint's approach, King Victor hid himself in a thick grove of trees. But as Patrick drew nearer, his own divine luminosity lit up the dark grove, and Victor, astonished by this miracle, revealed himself and begged Patrick to baptise him. Later, Victor gave his entire inheritance to the saint, to fund the building of a church. Later still, Victor became Bishop Victor of Rouen in France.

The story of Victor is not the only example of Patrick's divine luminescence that is mentioned in Jocelyn's Life of the saint. Patrick used his luminous fingers to provide a light whereby one of his charioteers could find their lost horses; and when the saint lost one of his teeth in a river, it could not be found until night fell: then its glowing form could be seen clearly. This tooth was later placed under the altar of a new church that was built nearby. Four of Patrick's followers were left behind to run the new foundation, which was called *Cluayn Fiacal*, or the Church of the Tooth.

The mention of Patrick's charioteer in the last paragraph is a reminder that, unlike the later Northumbrian saint, Cuthbert, Ireland's apostle did not wander around alone and on foot, trying to convert the people to Christianity, and trusting in God to protect him. Although Jocelyn insists that Patrick did not take to a chariot until he was too old to walk everywhere, the saint's vehicle features throughout Jocelyn's Life. Since Patrick cannot have been a young man, by the standards of his day, when he returned to Ireland, readers are entitled to suspect that Jocelyn may have overstated the saint's devotion to cross-country hiking.

Mounted on his chariot, and attended on his journey by so many devotees that he was able to leave large numbers of them behind to run the many churches he founded, some of the pagan Irish might have mistaken Patrick for a marauding petty king, intent on raiding the countryside and claiming booty other than just the souls of those he encountered. In one important respect, the saint was fundamentally different from a land-pirate of this type, however, even if we temporarily forget that he was a Christian missionary intent on raiding the hearts, and not the homes, of the people. Unlike the higher and lower kings of Ireland, Patrick, as a priest, was supposed to remain celibate, and so he could not have produced sons to be his supporters and successors; or daughters to marry to rival kings in order to cement alliances. Instead, Patrick relied for his succession on his nieces and nephews, and his spiritual children – his converts and comrades-in-arms in the fight against paganism.

The two sisters, Ethne and Fedella, whom Patrick had converted just before they died, were daughters of the aforementioned King Leogaire; and Glarcus, the giant whom Patrick had raised from the dead, had been a shepherd who had worked for the same monarch. Presumably Glarcus, with his huge frame and terrifying appearance, would have made a very effective shepherd, able to spot sheep-rustlers and other predators from miles away, and also able to scare them off before they got too near.

King Leogaire himself is supposed to have been rather more than just another petty Irish king: some accounts tell us that he was a High King of Ireland, entitled to use as his headquarters the Hill of Tara, located in modern County Meath: a part of this ancient site is known as the Fortress of Leogaire Mac Neill. Leogaire was a son of Niall of the Nine Hostages, another High King of Ireland, who is thought to have taken advantage of the comparative defencelessness of the communities in what we now call Great Britain, after they had ceased to be part of the Roman Empire.

Niall was able to form alliances with the Picts, the ancient occupants of what we now call Scotland, who were pagans like the Irish themselves (the Irish, confusingly, were called Scots at the time). The Scots and Picts joined together to raid the Roman Christians of Britain, and it may have been one of the raiding parties organised by Niall which had captured the teenage Patrick. In the *Letter to the Soldiers of Coroticus*, one of the writings attributed to him, Patrick mentions that these raiders also killed his father's farm-workers.

While petty kings like Victor and Milchu were frightened of Patrick, the powerful

Leogaire, son of Niall of the Nine Hostages, thought he could over-match the saint, and even eliminate him as a problem.

Even before Patrick had set foot on Irish soil, Leogaire was arranging to have him driven out of Ireland straight away, or killed when he landed. The saint's ship landed at the mouth of the River Bray in what is now County Wicklow, and Patrick was greeted by a hostile crowd. An attempt was made to set a savage dog on him, but the animal became paralysed at the sight of the saint. The same fate befell a gigantic man called Dichu, who was converted to Christianity on the spot. As his heart turned to Christ, the paralysis left him.

Evidently a man of some wealth and power, as well as a giant, Dichu soon became one of Patrick's most important allies and protectors, and he encouraged the saint to build a church by the Bray, on the site of his first miracles on Irish soil.

As if trying to live up to his father's name, 'Niall of the Nine Hostages', Leogaire, the pagan High King, retained hostages to guarantee the cooperation of all the local provincial chiefs. When he learned that Dichu and his entire family had gone over to Patrick's side, he forbade anyone to give water to any of his hostages from Dichu's household. When Leogaire refused to negotiate with either Patrick or Dichu on this matter, Patrick 'betook himself to his accustomed arms of prayer', and soon an angel appeared bearing drink for Dichu's people. After a few days, the angel also freed them, transporting them to safely by carrying them through the air.

Flying was a feature of a later clash between Leogaire and Patrick. One of the associates of the High King was a pagan priest who was regarded almost as a god on earth by Leogaire and his people. This man, called Lochu, could even fly through the air like an angel, but in his case this power came not from God but via 'the prince of darkness'. When Patrick witnessed this feat, he prayed that Lochu would suffer the fate of Icarus, and fall to earth. The saint's prayer was answered, and soon Lochu's shattered body was lying at Patrick's feet.

Leogaire was so exasperated by the death of Lochu that he came against Patrick with a military force, which included chariots and mounted soldiers. In response, the saint broke up the High King's warlike host with an earthquake and a shower of lightning-bolts. As if this wasn't enough, Patrick then called on the power of God to make Leogaire's surviving warriors go mad and fight against each other. By the end of this strange battle, forty-nine of Leogaire's men were lying dead, and the survivors only escaped with great difficulty. The High King himself got away to some kind of bolt-hole, with only four of his closest followers.

In the aftermath of the battle, Leogaire pretended to go over to Patrick's side, but in fact he went on to make several more attempts on the saint's life, and finally died a pagan. There are several different accounts of his death, but the most appealing one casts him as an ancient Irish Macbeth.

It had been prophesied that Leogaire would only die when he was between Eire and Alba, meaning Ireland and Scotland. This is like the prophecy of the weird sisters in Shakespeare's *Macbeth*, who tell the hero that he cannot be killed by anyone born of a woman.

Leogaire naturally thought that his prophecy meant that he could avoid death altogether by avoiding any sea-voyages. But like Macbeth's, the High King's prophecy spoke with a forked tongue. Leogaire hadn't realised that there were two mountains in Ireland called Eire and Alba, and when he passed between them he was struck by lightning and killed.

Saint Patrick contrasts with many other Christian saints in his use of his miraculous powers as military assets, as demonstrated in his battle with Leogaire, and in his extensive use of what might be called 'revenge miracles'. In these cases, he responded to an insult, an attack or just a disappointment, by, for instance, causing his opponents to be sucked straight down to hell. He also cursed rivers so that their fish-stocks would go down to almost nothing, and he saddled certain families with infertility, or with generations of political failure.

The picture of Saint Patrick riding around on a chariot, calling on God to cause earthquakes and unleash thunder-bolts against a heathen people, imparts an Old Testament grandeur to many tales of the saint, although parts of Jocelyn's account, and Patrick's own *Confessio,* hint at his deep humility and tendency to self-doubt.

Some say that Patrick retired from the Irish scene after his spectacular missionary efforts, and died and was buried at Glastonbury in England. Others say that he remained in Ireland, did not suffer martyrdom (despite the efforts of Leogaire and others) and sickened and died, as well he might, at the age of one hundred and twenty-three. He is said to lie under a heavy stone in the shadow of Down Cathedral in Downpatrick, Northern Ireland.

*The Chief Druid, from A Tour of Wales
by Thomas Pennant (1726-17)*

II. Brígíd

Ireland has three patron saints, Patrick being the most senior, and his contemporary Brigid being the only woman. The third member of Ireland's trio of patrons is Columba.

Brigid was often with Patrick, and had a role in his funeral, an occasion which included glowing angels among its guests.

As Patrick was nearing death, he was preaching a sermon near a graveyard, when 'a great light descended from heaven, and poured round a certain spot on the eastern side of the cemetery'. Brigid, 'the spotless Pearl of Hibernia' was in the congregation, and Patrick asked her what this might mean. Brigid said that the light was shining on the place where a great saint would be buried. Later, Brigid revealed to a nun called Ethembria that Patrick himself would be buried where the light had shone. Brigid also revealed to Ethembria that she had woven a linen shroud for the saint. When this was offered to Patrick, he received it with thanks. This, of course, was the shroud in which the saint was buried.

The incident related above, where Patrick deferred to Brigid's superior insight, is not unique in the old accounts of the lives of these two saints. Once, Patrick was at a place called Tailtiu, now known as Teltown in County Meath. A woman appeared there with a small child, and claimed that the child had been conceived under rather scandalous circumstances. She had gone to a bishop called Bron to be made a nun, but, she alleged, the bishop had seduced her. The child she had in tow was the the result of the seduction, and she now wanted to give it to its father.

Another bishop, called Mel, was present at Teltown, and he suggested that Brigid should be called in to sort out the rights and wrongs of the case. Mel added that Brigid, whom he seems to have assumed would settle the matter by a miracle, would not perform such a miracle in the presence of St Patrick. Patrick was happy to go along with this.

Brigid questioned Bron's accuser out of sight of Patrick, and the reluctant mother again named Bishop Bron as the father. Brigid told her she was lying, and her tongue swelled up, in effect stopping her mouth. The saint then took the unusual step of asking the child who its father was, even though the infant was far too young to talk. By a miracle, the child spoke, and pointed out his father, who turned out to be an ugly fellow who was sitting nearby.

At this, the people turned on the lying mother, saying she should be burned; but Brigid suggested penance instead, and the woman's swollen tongue returned to its normal size.

Another time when Patrick showed his respect for Brigid was when she appeared to be showing disrespect for him. At a place called Fionnabhair, Patrick showed his enthusiasm for preaching by delivering an explanation of the gospels that went on uninterrupted for three days. According to Jocelyn's account, the saint's discourse was so absorbing that the congregation believed that only one day had passed – nevertheless, Brigid, who was there, committed the apparently unforgivable crime of falling asleep.

Patrick instructed that she should be allowed to sleep on, and when she awoke of her own accord, he questioned her about her dreams. Yes, she had indeed dreamed, she assured him. In her dream, she had seen people in white clothes; but these had been followed by people in spotted clothes, then people clothed in black. At last, the people in her dream had been replaced by sheep, pigs, dogs and wolves, all fighting together. Patrick interpreted Brigid's dream as a vision of the then perfect state of the Irish church, followed by a premonition of its future decline.

Jocelyn asserts that Brigid's dream proved to be a true prophecy: whether he was right or wrong, the idea that the age of Patrick and Brigid was a golden one, populated by angelic people in white raiment, comes out clearly in this story.

In the Latin biography of Brigid by the seventh-century Irish monk Cogitosus, and in an anonymous hagiography written in the Irish language, the 'Pearl of Hibernia' demonstrates the boundless generosity which was a trait expected from popular rulers at this time, and which is bound to be a characteristic of the leading people of any age that can qualify as golden.

Brigid was the daughter of a druid called Dubthach, and it seems that she was expected to help on her father's farm, much as the daughters of hard-up Anglican parish priests in the eighteenth century would have fed the pigs and the chickens, collected eggs from the hen-house, milked the cow, and churned butter.

The saint's daily contact with farm-work gave her so many opportunities to give to the poor that, according to the anonymous Irish Life, her pagan father tried to sell her as a slave to the king of Leinster, since he regarded Brigid, his own daughter, as a thief. True to form, Brigid, who had been left outside to look after Dubthach's cart while he negotiated with the king, gave away a sword that was in the cart to a poor leper. Dubthach was furious, since the sword was worth the value of ten cows, and wasn't even his own – it belonged to another king. Now determined to leave Brigid behind as a slave, he rode off alone, only to find that, by a miracle, his daughter had been placed right behind him in his cart. Hearing about this, Dunlag, the king of Leinster to whom the druid had offered to sell his daughter, concluded that Brigid could never be bought or sold, and he sent her his own royal sword to replace the one she had given away.

Sometimes Brigid's generosity to

beggars, many of whom are identified in the sources as lepers, is so excessive that it seems almost miraculous in itself. Likewise, the demands some beggars make of her are a long way from the crust of bread or the few coins that beggars in stories usually ask for. One particularly optimistic leper asked for her best cow and her best calf. Realising that the calf was too young to make any kind of journey, the saint gave the leper her chariot and horses as well, so that the calf could ride in the chariot behind its new owner. There is a minor miracle connected with this story: the cow, which was not the calf's biological mother, accepted it as its own, and followed behind the chariot on foot to keep it company.

Although Brigid's generosity may have seemed insane at times, Dubthach's exasperation with his daughter was still unfair. Almost everything she gave away to the poor was miraculously replaced. Even when Brigid was acting as a shepherd, and seven of the sheep in her care were stolen, the flock was found to contain the original number of animals, when they were carefully counted, several times, at the end of the day.

Likewise, when the saint was cooking a sort of pork stew in a cauldron, she gave some of the meat to a poor dog; but when the meal was served up, the amount of pork was found to be just the same as if the dog had never begged at her kitchen door.

Brigid's father should have been more appreciative of the benefits the saint brought to his household, since nature, which always works in partnership with farmers, was as generous to Brigid as she herself was to poor people, and even animals. Once, when everyone else's ripe crops were ruined by torrential rain, Brigid enjoyed a dry and bountiful harvest. Likewise, when there was a shortage of milk, the saint was able to milk the same cow three times in one day, and get as much from it as three good cows could have been expected to produce in the same period. On another occasion, a river rose up out of its banks and swept away some cattle-rustlers who were making off with Brigid's personal cow.

The miracles associated with Brigid's generosity, and nature's many gifts to her, are a reminder that the Irish economy in the days of Patrick and Brigid was based around food production, and relied heavily on the contribution of the useful cow. These animals were used as currency, in a country of many small, scattered communities, some of them, the *raths*, fortified to some extent against raiders. Later, the design of the *rath* was adapted to monastic purposes, as monasteries were built in many places.

Much of Ireland in those days was covered with forests, bogs and mountains, and there were eighty or so petty kingdoms, each with its own royal family. The kings themselves were important elements in the religious hierarchy of pagan Ireland, and, as we have seen, druids such as Brigid's father often served in the courts of the petty kings.

Brigid's relationship with nature has led some to suggest that the saint never existed as a real person, but was in fact a carefully fabricated Christian version of one of the most powerful goddesses in the Irish pagan pantheon.

Danu or Dana, also known as Anu and Brigit, was a pagan goddess of fertility, who was also associated with fire. The *Tuatha De Danann* were so called because they were the children or people of Danu. These were ancient invaders of Ireland, remembered in myths and legends as beings with god-like powers. The legends relate that when their power over the island faltered, they did not die out, but went underground and became the aforementioned *aes sidhe*, fairy-like dwellers in mounds.

The ancient belief in Brigit, the pagan fire-goddess, is perhaps reflected in the story that there was once an eternal flame, tended by virgins in honour of the Christian Brigid, at Kildare in the east of Ireland. This Irish Christian version of the eternal flame of the Roman vestal virgins was located at the abbey Brigid founded at Kildare, where she was the abbess. The fire was fuelled with oak, and many shrines to St Brigid were built under oak trees. In his book *The Religion of the Ancient Celts*, J.A. MacCulloch suggested that these new Christian shrines to St Brigid might have replaced older shrines to her pagan namesake. The replacement of pagan shrines and temples with Christian churches happened in many parts of Europe. The church of Santa Maria sopra Minerva in Rome is so-called because it was once thought that it had been built on the remains of a shrine to the Roman goddess Minerva.

Brigid's link with fire also comes out in several miracle-stories about her. As a child, she was trapped, sleeping, in a burning house, but when the locals ran to see what had happened, they found that both the girl and the house were not even scorched. Flames were also seen over her head, or over places she visited, these being reminiscent of the flames that appeared on the heads of the apostles at Pentecost (Acts 2), and the pillar of fire that led the Israelites through the wilderness by night (Exodus 13: 21).

The saint's connection with both wood and fire are re-stated in the story of a miracle that happened when she was being consecrated as a nun. She happened to reach down and touch an ash beam, which immediately turned into a beam made of acacia wood. Although the church where this happened burned down three times, the acacia beam was always found intact in the ruins.

Like Brigid, St Patrick also has equivalents among the characters described in Ireland's pagan legends. Indeed Cuchulain, the so-called Hound of Ulster, the greatest of the old mythical heroes of Ireland, rides around in a chariot and wreaks havoc among his enemies in a manner very similar to Patrick's.

Patrick even meets Cuchulain, in a story in a twelfth-century volume called *The Book of the Dun Cow*. In this episode, Patrick summons the Hound of Ulster out of hell, and encounters him on the Plain of Mac Indoc. This is all part of Patrick's plan to convert a local king, Laery mac Neill. Cuchulain does his part, and describes the pains of hell to the king, having first arrived on a powerful gust of wind, and emerged, huge and fearsome on his chariot, from a thick mist.

In fact St Patrick features in a number of Irish legends which are not hagiographies, in which he is able to rub shoulders with pagan elements and characters. In a medieval tale, the saint and his followers are charmed by the music of a man called Cascorach, a harpist who is the son of one of the *Tuatha De Danann*. The saint remarks that the harper's song is 'infested' with a 'fairy spell', but is forced to admit that it sounds like music from heaven itself. Elsewhere, the saint is similarly charmed by tales of the legendary Celtic hero Finn MacCool, but protests that he cannot spend all his time listening to such stories, though he might like to, because he has his religious duties to attend to.

During the time of Patrick, Ethne, an ancient being who, like Cascorach's father, was one of the *Tuatha*, found herself stranded in the world of mortals. She wandered into a monastery, was eventually baptised by St Patrick, and became a nun.

One day, while she was praying, she thought she could hear the voices of her fairy friends and relatives calling out for her. This caused such turmoil in her mind that she fell into a swoon, and soon died. The tale of Ethne's sad end suggests that the Irish myth-makers were prepared to entertain the idea that the strange parallel universe of the *Tuatha De Danaan* was still able to exist alongside the conflicting reality of an Ireland that was rapidly becoming Christian.

The misty mirror-world to which Ethne found herself unable to return is similar in some respects to those elements of the Christian model of the universe that saints like Patrick and Brigid were able to see, while their less saintly followers had to take such things on trust. These saints were able to perceive angels, demons and other beings that were invisible to most people, to see important contemporary events at a distance, to predict future events, and to catch glimpses of the contrasting eternities of heaven and hell.

The idea of parallel universes, and the ability to see things that others can't, have been taken up by modern writers of science fiction, and even by main-stream scientists. In Ray Bradbury's SF short stories *The*

Martian Chronicles, all the native Martians are understood to have died shortly after the arrival of the humans from earth, yet certain humans do encounter them, and are able to see into their lost world.

For many writers, as we have seen, St Brigid's identity blurs into that of the pagan goddess Brigit. In the Irish Life of the saint, she also stands in for the Virgin Mary.

There was a meeting of no less than twenty-seven Christian saints at Leinster, where a Bishop Ibor told the assembly that he had had a dream about the Virgin Mary. In his dream, he had seen the Virgin, and a cleric had pointed her out to Ibor 'as the Mary who will walk among you'. At that point in Ibor's sermon, Brigid arrived, and the bishop, who had evidently never met her before, declared that she was the Mary he had seen in his dream.

An important respect in which Brigid did not resemble the pagan goddess Brigit is that Brigid, like Patrick, remained a virgin, whereas the goddess had a number of children. Indeed when Ruadan, her son by her consort Bres, was killed, Brigit's wailing is said to have been the first mourning wail heard in Ireland.

In the Irish Life of Brigid, the saint's

resistance to an attempt to marry her off, and thus compromise her virginity, turns into another opportunity for her to show her miraculous powers and her trade-mark generosity. When a suitor, Dubthach moccu Lugair, who shared a name with her father, came to call, Brigid told him to step into the wood behind her father's house, where he would find a more willing future wife. To help the young man in his wooing, the saint blessed his face and his speech, so that both his looks and his words would be more attractive.

But Brigid's brothers were annoyed that the family was to be deprived of the dowry Dubthach the suitor would have brought, and they mocked their sister. One of them, Bacene, said that her beautiful eyes were bound to attract another suitor. At this, Brigid poked out one of her own eyes, thus following the instruction of Jesus:

And if thine eye offend thee, pluck it out, and cast it from thee: it is better for thee to enter into life with one eye, rather than having two eyes to be cast into hell fire.

(Matthew 18:9, KJV)

Following this shocking act, Brigid cursed her brother Bacene, saying that both his own eyes would soon burst.

The old authors' insistence that Brigid, Patrick and many other saints remained virgins, and in fact the medieval Christian obsession with virginity in general, is not palatable for many modern readers; but the story of Brigid's mild rejection of her suitor is a reminder that, by remaining celibate, these saints were not necessarily turning their backs on the kind of devoted, passionate relationship that modern people hope to get out of marriage, or even just regular dating. In many societies at the level of civilisation that early Christian Ireland had reached, marriages were arranged as practical deals between families, and romantic love was not regarded as an essential part of the arrangement at all. The woman thus married could very quickly be saddled with constant pregnancies and many children, and she might never be able to attain to the kind of independence and influence that Brigid enjoyed. A man like Patrick might have had to take on dynastic family responsibilities if he had married: he may have had to build up a stable of sons, who would have wanted wars to fight and wives to wed, and daughters he would have been expected to marry off to boys in neighbouring families, to forge alliances and gain dowries. In such a life, there may not have been any time for converting pagans, founding monasteries, carrying out the duties of a priest, and continuing a meaningful conversation with God through prayer, study and contemplation.

Although she is associated with generosity, Brigid, like Patrick, could also deliver effective curses, as she did in the case of her unfortunate brother who, we are told, really did go blind when his eyes burst right out of his head, as his sister had prophesied.

Once, Brigid was walking by the river Inny when a nun presented her with a gift of fruit, in a basket made of bark. As was her wont, Brigid immediately gave the fruit away to some lepers. The nun who had given Brigid the fruit objected, just like the saint's father, who also objected to her giving things away to lepers. In response, Brigid cursed the nun's fruit-trees so that, though they remained alive and had green leaves on them in season, they never bore fruit again.

Although it may seem cruel of Brigid to

have done so, the cursing of fruit trees has a good precedent in the gospels. Jesus curses a fig tree when he is hungry and it fails to provide him with fruit to eat, even though, in the gospel of Mark, it is stated that it was not the right season for the tree to have any figs on it in any case (Mark 11: 12-25; also Matthew 21: 18-19).

Saint Patrick also delivered many curses, and seems to have specialised in cursing rivers so that they would produce few or no fish. These stories may be Christian versions of old local legends originally dreamed up to explain, for instance, why a particular river had few if any fish in it, or why the trees of a particular orchard never bore fruit, in the days before science could come up with more down-to-earth explanations.

The exact opposite of the story of Brigid's curse on the nun's orchard is a tale that follows it in the Irish Life of the saint. Here, a woman identified as a 'virgin' (probably another nun) gives Brigid a large quantity of apples and sloes, which she promptly gives away to some lepers. This time, the original giver is not annoyed, and the saint blesses a tree in her garden, which goes on to produce both sloes and apples together, even though it is neither an apple tree nor a sloe tree or bush, but an alder. The author of the Irish Life assures us that the trees descended from this miraculous alder bore the same strange combination of fruit for many years.

Like Patrick, Brigid also performed many healing miracles, and the story of one of these, as related in the Irish Life, also connects to the saint's many acts of generosity.

Yet another leper was hectoring Brigid for the gift of a cow, refusing to go away unless she gave him one. When he threatened to try for a cow elsewhere, the saint offered him a miraculous cure instead. Rather like a memorable character in the 1979 British comedy film *The Life of Brian*, the leper protested that, if he were cured, he would make less money from begging. The physical pain he was suffering because of his illness eventually persuaded him, however, that a cure would be preferable. It is interesting that this cure was effected without the saint having to touch the leper – she merely blessed a cup of water that was then used to wash him: this banished the leprosy forever. At this point in the story, the leper's character changed, along with his health: he stopped being an annoying beggar who tried even the patience of a saint, and became her humble and devoted woodsman.

Brigid effected other cures by giving miraculous healing powers to well-water, water that she had turned into milk, water mixed with her own blood, and water she had used to wash her own feet. She also cured four nuns of Cul Fobair in Galway by washing their feet, though none of them had health problems specific to their feet at all: one was a leper, one was possessed by a demon, one was blind, and the last was suffering from paralysis.

Like Jesus, Brigid also cured people involuntarily, when she herself may have been unaware that a cure was happening at all. The cure she effected with a mixture of water and her own blood happened when she was travelling with two girls who had been dumb from birth. The saint fell and cut her head on a stone in a stream, and instructed the girls to wash their necks in the resulting mixture. But one of them was cured already, and she was able to tell Brigid that she had brought about her own cure a little earlier by kneeling in the tracks the saint's cart had left behind on the road.

Jesus affected a similar cure to Brigid's cart-track miracle, as if involuntarily, when a sick woman touched the hem of his garment (Matthew 9, 20).

Like Patrick, with his glowing fingers, Brigid also performed miracles that were incredibly handy, because they solved problems that cropped up at certain times. She healed at least three sick people who were being carried around in carts, so that the carts could be used for something else. She also cured the whole family of a man she found working alone in a field, who told her that all his close relatives were ill. This miracle points to the fact that, like the land controlled by Brigid's father, much cultivated land in Ireland was then tended by families working together.

Many of Brigid's miracles resembled those of her colleague St Patrick, though on average they were less punitive and smaller in scale. As we have seen, the saint also showed herself able to replicate miracles performed by Jesus, although the best of these does not resemble a miracle from the gospels, but from the apocryphal Gospel of Pseudo-Matthew, also known as the Infancy Gospel of Matthew. Although much read in medieval times, this gospel never made it into the 'final cut' of the New Testament, and was probably written hundreds of years after the latest parts of that book.

On this occasion, Brigid had come home from working in the fields soaked to the skin after a rain-storm, and entered a room where the sun was making its way through gaps in the wall. The sun-beams looked like solid horizontal poles, and Brigid proceeded to hang her wet clothes on them.

The equivalent miracle from Pseudo-Matthew involves the infant Jesus actually sitting on a sunbeam.

Hagiographers sometimes describe the deaths of saints in great detail: the details often hint at the kind of life the saint has led, and his or her expectations or intimations about the after-life. Dying saints, whether they perish as martyrs, or from natural causes, often give memorable final words of advice to their followers, re-state their dedication to God, make moving final confessions, see visions, and sometimes even perform last-minute miracles, or are inspired with the spirit of prophecy.

Neither the Irish Life of Brigid, nor the Life written in Latin by Cogitosus, give us much detail on the death of Brigid. One story that emerges, however, is that of St Ninnidh, who tended her in her final days, and gave her the last rites. It is said that, since he had touched Brigid with his right hand, he had that hand encased in metal so that it would remain pure and blessed. Thereafter, he became known as Ninnidh of the Clean Hand.

*Statue of St Brendan by Tigue O'Donoghue
at Fenit, Co. Kerry; photo by Mr Charco*

III. Columba and Brendan

Once, the aforementioned Celtic hero Finn
MacCool was hunting deer. When he had
trapped a deer by a river, he sent in his
faithful hound Bran to kill it, but she would
not. The whole hunting party was amazed at
the dog's disobedience, but Finn 'betook
himself to his gift of knowledge' and
prophesied that at some point in the future,
St Columba would bless the place, and make
it a sanctuary.

It was not only a legendary hero from the
misty past who prophesied the coming of our
next saint. Once, when St Patrick grew angry
with a river, he only imposed a curse on one
half of it: he said that Columba, 'a son of
life', would need fish from the other half.
Patrick also blessed a man called Conall Mac
Neill, only because he prophesied that
Columba would later be born into his tribe.

A similar story about Columba's strange
relationship with the past relates how a giant

skull was once brought to him. While he sat there holding the skull, like Shakespeare's Hamlet, the saint's divine insight told him that it was the skull of his ancestor Cormac mac Airt, father-in-law of Finn MacCool. Unlike the skull of Yorick in Shakespeare's play, Cormac's then started to talk to his saintly descendant. It claimed, in effect, that he, Cormac, had been spared the pains of hell, not just because he had been a good man (for a pagan) but also because it was known that Columba 'would be of his seed'. And so he had spent his time in purgatory, and not hell, waiting for Columba to pray for his release.

Whether they were ever really spoken or not, the prophecies about Columba that appear in stories of the Irish saints tend to point up his importance, if nothing else. They are especially impressive in view of the fact that Columba's impact was felt mainly in what we now call Scotland, and not so much in his native Ireland. Although he may have been a much younger contemporary of Brigid, who sometimes seems like a mythical being, Columba himself is certainly a real historical figure. He is named in a variety of early sources, and his biography was written by Adomnan, the abbot of Iona, an abbey

Columba himself founded. Adomnan was born less than thirty years after Columba himself died.

Although Columba seems to have had a crucial role in the religious and secular politics of his time, the biography by Adomnan gives few practical details, preferring to concentrate on the saint's many miracles and prophecies. As Richard Sharpe suggests in the introduction to his 1995 translation of Adomnan's biography, the abbot's account was probably written for readers who were already familiar with the more mundane parts of Columba's CV. A speculative outline of the less miraculous elements of Columba's career can, however, be assembled, from a range of sources, including Adomnan's little book.

The saint is supposed to have been born some time around the year 521 A.D., into the highest level of the Irish aristocracy of the time. He could count himself as one of the Ui Neill, the descendants of the aforementioned king, Niall of the Nine Hostages. At some point, perhaps because of the attraction he felt to the church, he acquired the nick-name Columcille, meaning 'church dove'. This evokes the image of a peaceful bird nesting in some part of a church building; but the bearer of the nickname was not always at peace, and seems to have been too active and restless to spend much time in one place.

Little is known about Columba's life in Ireland until the year 563, when he left his native land at the age of about forty-two. Abbot Adomnan, who is always concerned to put a positive spin on Columba's life, says that an attempt was made to excommunicate the saint at a synod at Teltown in Meath. Adomnan says that there were 'pardonable and very trifling reasons' why some thought that Columba should be cut off from the church, but others have constructed a darker back-story for this synod.

It is asserted that St Finnian of Moville, one of Columba's spiritual mentors, owned a marvellous book which contained a number of spiritual classics, including all the psalms of the Old Testament, and St Jerome's Latin translation of the Gospels. Finnian allowed his protégé to borrow this book, but forbade him to make a copy. Columba's 'pardonable and very trifling' transgression may have been his decision to copy the book, despite Finnian's prohibition. This the saint did by staying behind in church after the last service every night, and working away with his quill.

He was able to see what he was doing, because he could make his fingers glow – a miraculous gift he shared with St Patrick.

When he found out about Columba's illicit copy of his book, Finnian was enraged, and brought the case to King Diarmit at Tara. Speaking in his own defence, the saint asserted that Finnian's book was none the worse for his copying it, and implied that, if they were not spread abroad 'among the tribes' by the process of copying, the 'divine words in that book' would be lost when the book itself perished.

Despite the saint's eloquence, Diarmit found against Columba, saying that Finnian should keep the new copy, much as a cow would keep its calf. It was now Columba's turn to be enraged. The saint's mood was not improved when a prince called Curnan, who had been placed under his protection, was killed by agents of the same King Diarmit.

The unfortunate Curnan had been a son of the king of Connaght, and when the friction between Diarmit and this king sparked into the battle of Culdreihmne, Columba fought alongside the forces of Connaght against King Diarmit and his army. It may be that the synod at Teltown refrained from excommunicating Columba on condition that he go into exile as a missionary, and convert to Christianity the same number of people who had been killed at Culdreihmne. This, according to some versions of Columba's life, is what brought him to Iona, which he used as a bridgehead for his holy invasion of what we now call Scotland.

This story of a war, or at least a battle, partly fought because of a dispute over a book, is a reminder of one of the problems that used to beset Christian monks, priests, missionaries and believers in general in those days. Christianity is a religion of the book, and in many cases, when missionaries brought the Word to a new community, they also brought literacy to them for the first time. But in those days the technology of reading and writing was expensive and cumbersome, and whereas today we might casually put a book into a pocket or a rucksack, the precious books of the early middle ages had to be treated with great care, like human organs destined for transplant, or fuel-rods for a nuclear power-plant.

Another story that shows Columba's attachment to books concerns a rich miser called Longarad of Kilgarrow, whose sumptuous library was coveted by the saint.

When Columba came to visit, Longarad hid his books away; and in retaliation the saint asked God to make the books utterly useless to anybody after Longarad's death. In this way, Columba hoped to negate the books' value as an heirloom; but there is an ironic twist to the story which shows how even a mighty saint can sometimes be wrong-footed. Terrified by what amounted to a curse from Columba, Longarad gave all his books to the saint, but the moment the old miser died, they became illegible. Because of their association with Columba, however, these unreadable books remained 'incorrupt', meaning that time and age could not touch them, and after many years there was no 'change or defilement or dimness upon those letters'.

In a story that probably became attached to Columba's legend some time after Adomnan had written his Life of the saint, we learn that on leaving Ireland he had sworn never to see that island or any of its people again, nor to tread its soil, or eat or drink anything from there. When, inevitably, he had to return, he stood, blindfolded, on a sod of earth that had been brought from Scotland, and he had with him enough food and drink to keep him going during his visit, without his having to eat or drink anything Irish.

The story of Columba cunningly getting round his vow, and also Columba's speech defending his actions in copying Finnian's book, both come from a compilation of stories about the saint written in Irish by one Manus O'Donnell, and completed in 1532. In part of the introduction to their 1918 translation of O'Donnell's book, Andrew O'Kelleher and Gertrude Schoepperle describe how 'the present Life is overlaid with a thousand poetic incidents gathered from pagan and Christian times'. These include 'episodes familiar in the lives of other saints, in romances of troubadours and Arthurian knights'. The editors of the 1918 book imply that it is up to the reader to decide if these additions are encumbrances – like barnacles on the hull of a ship – or adornments, like the jewels on an elaborate case fashioned for a holy relic.

It should not be imagined that, though he was leaving Ireland, Columba was entirely cutting himself off from his own people – the people who spoke the Celtic language he had learned as a child. In Columba's day, there was such a well-established Irish presence in the west of Scotland that the area, and part of the north-east of Ireland, formed a single kingdom called Dal Riada.

East of Dal Riada, in Columba's day, were the kingdoms of a separate people, the aforementioned Picts, who lived in what historians now call 'Pictland'. Little is known about these people, who had fought against the Romans, and had probably gained the Latin name '*picti*' because of their habit of painting or tattooing their skins.

Although authors like Sally M. Foster in her 2014 book *Picts, Gaels and Scots* suggest that the Picts were themselves Celts, like the Irish with whom they then shared Scotland, their Celtic language had evolved separately from that of Columba's countrymen, who could no longer understand them. Despite the language barrier, and many other problems, the pagan Picts were an important target for Columba's missionary efforts.

As well as hinting at a few of the practical details of Columba's remarkable career, Adomnan's Life of the saint offers many small glimpses of everyday existence in the remote, watery kingdom of Dal Riada during this equally remote time. In fact historians regard Adomnan's book as the most important written source that has survived from the period. An example of how historians have long been reading between the lines of this work is to be found in the introduction to William Reeves's 1857 edition of Adomnan, where he plunders Adomnan's *Columba* and other texts, gathering scraps of information about the monastic Rule by which Columba and his monks lived.

In Adomnan, we learn of monks doing heavy manual work, and being comforted by the mere presence of Columba, not just in the flesh, but sometimes in the spirit. Once, seeing some monks toiling near his own abbey, the saint approached them, this time in the flesh, and promised them that no snakes, nor any poisonous reptiles, would ever be seen on Iona again. We also read about monks collecting sticks to make a house – presumably a wattle-and daub house – with earth walls reinforced by 'wattles' or large-scale basket-work.

There is also a reminder in the tales of Columba of the ancient habit of killing and eating almost all of the pigs belonging to a settlement, in autumn, when they had fed well on seasonal nuts and fruit, because they could not be fed adequately during the winter months. This practice is central to the story of a rich man called Federach, whom Columba had asked to protect a noble Pictish exile called Terain. When Federach had Terain killed, the saint promised that the faithless man would die before he could take part in the annual autumn pork blowout. Sure enough, Federach died suddenly just before the first morsel of pork reached his mouth that year.

In those days, in Ireland and what we now call Scotland, the status of a family was evidently measured in cattle, although of course they also kept pigs, and sheep. Rather like Brigid, who gave away cows to beggars, Columba would cause cattle to multiply exponentially in the corrals of those Christian souls who were loyal and faithful to him and his cause. Adomnan's Life also tells us about men like one Cormac, who set out to 'discover a desert in the ocean', i.e. to find a remote island on which to live as a hermit, or perhaps found a monastery as Columba had on Iona, and later on other islands. Using his power of prophecy, Columba saw that Cormac would land on one of the Orkney islands, off the northernmost tip of mainland Scotland. Fortunately the saint was friends with Brude, a king of the Picts, who was able to ensure that Cormac was received hospitably by the Orcadians.

Brude had good reason to cooperate with the saint, although he was a pagan when he first encountered Columba. Their first meeting happened after the saint had travelled to Brude's royal fortress. At first, the king refused to open his gates to Columba. In response to this inhospitable display, the saint merely laid his hand upon the gates: their bolts slid back, they opened, and Columba and his followers stepped inside. When he heard about this powerful miracle, the king rushed out to greet his visitors with the greatest respect.

As well as visiting many islands, and also diverse places on the British mainland, Columba received visitors to his own island of Iona. These included the famous Irish saint, Brendan the Navigator, whose adventures are recounted in an eighth-century book called the *Navigatio Brendani*. These stories are so fantastic that the *Navigatio* sometimes reads more like science fiction or fantasy than a series of tales from the life of a saint.

In the *Navigatio* Brendan, and the monks who accompany him in his boat made of hides, visit an island where there are so many sheep that it is hard to see the ground between them: and the sheep in this place are also as large as oxen. The travellers also encounter a fish so gigantic that they accidentally camp out on its back, thinking that it is an island. When they make a fire to cook their breakfast, the fish, called Jasconius, ducks under the waves to escape the heat and extinguish the fire.

The voyagers also see a crystal column in the ocean, so tall that they cannot see the top of it. After marvelling at this strange object, the monks approach an island which is populated by hideous, dark, hairy blacksmiths, who throw giant chunks of burning slag at them. Readers who like to try to detect the mundane truth behind such traveller's tales might speculate that Brendan's crystal column was actually an iceberg, and that the flaming island of the blacksmiths was an active volcano.

Some have suggested that the tales of Brendan's voyages are mythologised accounts of real travels that took the saint around the coasts of the British Isles, up into the Arctic Circle, and west as far as Greenland and even North America. To show that a voyage to the New World might have been possible for Brendan, in 1976 the explorer Tim Severin set out from Ireland in a reproduction of Brendan's boat, and, after over a year and many pauses, managed to reach Newfoundland.

If Brendan never got quite that far, then the stories in the *Navigatio* might be distant echoes of memories of journeys around the watery kingdom of Dal Riada, where there were many different islands, some occupied by monks, as are some of the islands described in the *Navigatio*.

The most bizarre of all Brendan's encounters is with no less a personage than Judas Iscariot, the disciple who betrayed Jesus. In the *Navigatio*, Judas is sitting on a rugged rock in the sea, enjoying a day's respite from the torments of hell.

Compared to his encounters in some of the places that feature in the *Navigatio Brendani*, Brendan's visit to Columba's island of Iona was unremarkable. All that happened was that, while Columba was celebrating the Mass for Brendan and some other saintly visitors, the sailor-saint saw 'a ball of fire like a comet burning very brightly on the head of Columba'.

The island of Iona, which an experienced sailor like Brendan would surely have had no problem reaching, is less than four miles from end to end, measured from the north-east to the south-west. It lies less than a mile off the south-west tip of the much larger island of Mull, which, on modern maps, seems to reach out to Iona with a rough-hewn hand. Iona and Mull are two of Scotland's seven hundred and ninety offshore islands. Many of these are to be found among the Hebrides, an archipelago which lies where the west-pointing 'face' of Scotland seems to fragment into sea-lochs and scattered islands, much as a sand-castle will break up under the onslaught of the incoming tide.

Much of the most significant portion of Columba's life was based on Iona, so it is hardly surprising that many of the stories Adomnan has to tell about the saint concern the sea, and islands, and the lochs that are such a spectacular feature of the north and west of Scotland. Indeed, if we were to allocate two of the four elements to St Brigid, they would perhaps be Earth and Fire, whereas Columba's would be Earth and Water.

Columba's most spectacular water-based miracle took place nearly a hundred miles north-east of Iona, at Loch Ness. Here the saint and some attendant monks came upon a pagan burial in progress at the edge of the loch. The mourners told the saint that they were burying a man who had been swimming in the loch, and been bitten to death by the famous monster that some say still dwells in its waters. Some of the people at the impromptu funeral had rowed out to the unfortunate swimmer in a boat, but he was literally dead in the water by the time they got to him. In a ghoulish detail, Adomnan tells us that the best these would-be rescuers could then do for the monster's victim was to fish him out with a hook.

If any of Columba's followers had been standing near the edge of the water while this sorry tale was being told, some would no doubt have moved up further onto dry land; but the saint was determined to cross the loch despite the monster, rather than go round: Loch Ness is, after all, over twenty miles long.

The saint ordered a faithful follower called Lugne Mocumin to swim across and fetch a small boat that he could see moored on the far shore. Lugne stripped off and dived in without any hesitation.

If this was the same Lugne Mocumin, then he had first come to Saint Columba as a young man suffering from constant bleeding from the nose. The saint blessed him by squeezing his nostrils together with the fingers of his right hand, and from that moment he never had another nose-bleed.

The hunger of the monster who now shared the loch with Lugne had evidently not been satisfied by the chunk he had taken out of his last human victim. This grisly snack had merely whetted his appetite, and when he sensed Lugne swimming above him, where he lay at the bottom of the loch, he surfaced, let out a terrifying roar, and began to chase Columba's disciple.

When 'Nessie' was within a spear's length of his prey, Columba, standing on the bank, made the sign of the Cross in the air, and commanded the monster to stop and go back. This he did, so quickly that it was as if he were being pulled back by invisible ropes.

This demonstration of the power of the Cross made the heathens who had watched it understand the superiority of the Christian God. Lugne himself went on to become the prior of a monastery on Nave Island, near Islay, to the south of Iona.

Adomnan's account of Columba's encounter with the Loch Ness Monster, which is now over thirteen hundred years old, is regarded as the first written record of that notorious creature.

It might be said that by commanding the hapless Lugne to risk his neck in Loch Ness, Columba was being reckless with another man's life, and showing no personal courage. The saint did, however, face up to many grave dangers in his own right, though it must be said that he was always protected by the miraculous powers God had granted him.

One of the poor men Columba had enriched by causing his cattle to multiply (in this case from a mere five to an impressive one hundred and five) was called Columban. He lived at Ardnamurchan, still a wild and unspoilt place on the western coast of Scotland. Having grown rich, Columban was repeatedly harassed by a robber called Joan (in this case a man's name), who raided his house and, with his henchmen, carried off anything of value. On the third occasion when Joan and his associates plundered Columban's house, Saint Columba, alone, intercepted them as they were carrying their booty back to their boat.

The saint criticised the actions of the robbers in no uncertain terms, and told them to leave their plunder behind. They mocked him and laughed at him, jumped into their boat, and were soon out on the sea. But if they had looked back, they would have seen Columba wading out, raising his hands up to heaven, invoking the name of Jesus, and standing knee-deep in the water for some time.

When he had finished his prayer, Columba returned to dry land and sat down with his companions. He told them that all the robbers they had just seen getting into their boat would soon die. 'This day a furious storm shall proceed from a cloud, which you will soon see rising in the north,' said the saint, though it was a clear day; and sure enough, Joan and his partners in crime were lost in a sudden storm, between the islands of Mull and Colonsay.

The story of the fate of Joan, as told by Adomnan, has some curious details. The robbers are out for Columban's portable treasure, and not his real wealth: his hundred plus cows. Presumably none of these animals could have been fitted into their boat. It may be that the Joan gang could not have rustled any of Columban's cattle, though Ardnamurchan is part of the Scottish mainland, because the robbers themselves were based on one of the nearby islands.

Joan himself seems not to have been a

mere peasant turned crook: Adomnan goes out of his way to tell us that he was a 'son of Conall, son of Domnall, sprung from the royal tribe of Gabran'. Perhaps many people could have claimed such a heritage, and not all of them could make a living by legitimate means.

Columba's treatment of the gang, though it culminates with their deaths by something like one of St Patrick's curses, is also comparatively restrained. There is no suggestion that the saint intervenes at all until Joan robs his friend three times, and even then he gives the robbers an opportunity to drop their ill-gotten gains before he calls on Jesus to punish them.

The saint's treatment of another robber was even milder. Using his miraculous ability to see things so far away that his mundane senses could not have perceived them, Columba became aware that a man called Erc Mocudruidi, from the island of Colonsay, was hiding just inland on the island of Mull, waiting for night. 'He strives to hide himself among the sand hills during the daytime under his boat, which he covers with hay,' the saint explained to two monks called Lugbe and Silnan. At night, Erc would sail over 'to the little island where our young seals are brought forth and nurtured', kill as many seals as his boat would hold, then sail back to Mull.

Of course Lugbe and Silnan found Erc hiding under his boat, just as their abbot had predicted, and hauled him up before Columba. The saint questioned him, and told him that he had no need to steal the abbey's seals to eat: the monks would happily give him some of their sheep as a substitute.

It might be supposed that Columba would have been rather more angry about the continuing presence of druids, the pagan priests, in Scotland and Ireland at the time, than he was about thieves. But even members of the heathen opposition to the saint's Christian preaching were treated with restraint.

A powerful druid called Broichan, who lived in the territory of King Brude, had a female slave whom Columba wanted to see released. He warned the druid that if he did not free her, he would soon die: but this time Columba's threat was not carried out.

The saint was walking by Loch Ness when he picked up a white pebble and said that the stone would heal many heathens in that kingdom. He added that at that very moment the stubborn Broichan was being attacked by an invisible angel, who had broken the glass cup from which he had been drinking. The angel, who visited the druid at King Brude's court, also caused the slave-owner's chest to become horribly tight, so that he could hardly breathe, and seemed half-dead. 'We will wait here,' the saint concluded. 'The druid has freed the girl, and the king has sent messengers asking us to go there and help Broichan.'

Soon the expected messengers arrived, begging for Columba's help. But the saint merely gave them the white pebble he had found. 'If the pebble is dipped in Broichan's drinking-water,' the saint explained, 'he will get better as soon as he drinks it: as long as he still intends to free the slave-girl.'

Back at Brude's court, Columba's instructions were followed to the letter. The druid was not only restored to perfect health: it was found that the stone itself floated in the water, 'contrary to the laws of nature'.

King Brude kept the stone in his personal treasury, and it effected many miraculous cures; but whenever a person who was destined to die asked for the pebble-cure, the stone could never be found. This is exactly what happened on the day that King Brude himself died.

Like many of the saints, Columba knew when his own death was imminent: he did not need the disappearance of a miraculous white pebble to tell him when his time had come.

Adomnan implies that as well as knowing when death was approaching, Columba was even able to influence exactly when it was going to happen. Close to the time of his death, he used his chariot to visit some monks who were working on the west side of Iona. He told them that he had wanted to die during Easter, which had just passed, but he had put off his time till the Easter festivities had finished, so that his brother monks would not be plunged into mourning at what should have been a joyous season.

A few days after he had confided this information to the monks, Columba's face 'appeared as if suffused with a ruddy glow' while he was celebrating Mass on a Sunday. He had seen an angel hovering near him in the oratory, though nobody else could see it. The saint explained to his followers that the angel had come for his soul. Six days later, at midnight, when Saturday became Sunday, Columba died.

Earlier, while the saint was resting by a

rugged stone cross on Iona, on the day when he knew he would die at midnight, a white pack-horse the monks used to carry milk appeared and rested its head on Columba's chest. The horse wept bitterly, wailed and foamed at the mouth. The saint explained to his companion that God himself had given the horse the knowledge of his imminent passing, and allowed it to mourn for him while he was still alive.

Although the activity had caused him a lot of trouble decades earlier, Columba spent the end of his last day copying out the psalms. When he had reached the line 'They that seek the Lord shall want no manner of thing that is good' (Psalm 34) he stopped, and instructed that a monk called Baithene should continue the copying after his death.

That night, as he had predicted, he died in his sleep, lying as usual on a bare flag-stone, with another stone for his pillow.

17th Century Austrian statue of Oswald

IV. Oswald and Aidan

In Adamnan's account, the period immediately before Columba's death is much more full of interesting episodes than the period just before Brigid's death, about which the earliest sources are almost completely silent. According to Adomnan, one of the things Columba did during his surprisingly busy last day on earth was to climb a hill overlooking the monastery of Iona, and make the following prophecy:

'Small and mean though this place is, yet it shall be held in great and unusual honour, not only by Scotic kings and people, but also by the rulers of foreign and barbarous nations, and by their subjects; the saints also even of other churches shall regard it with no common reverence.'

Like all of Columba's prophecies, this one turned out to be true; though it must be said that in the saint's own time, the island where he had founded his monastery had already achieved a prestige quite disproportionate to its modest size, and its location near the extreme outer edge of Europe. The saint was perhaps constructing his prophecy by extrapolating from what he had already seen.

A striking indication of the respect accorded to Columba and the island-headquarters of his mission was the crowning of Aedan mac Gabrain on the island in 574. The coronation ceremony was conducted by Columba himself, and it is the first Christian coronation known to have happened in Great Britain. Aedan was a warrior king of Dal Riada, who waged war in the Orkneys, the Isle of Man, Ireland and Scotland. The king confirmed his respect for Columba and Iona by sending trophies he had won in battle to Columba's abbey. He finally met defeat at the Battle of Degsastan (perhaps fought at Liddesdale in the north-east of Scotland). The victor in this battle was King Eathelfrith of Bernicia, the father of Oswald, our fourth Celtic saint.

King Aedan was also buried on Iona, and according to a sixteenth-century account, another forty-seven Scottish kings were later buried there, including Macbeth, the anti-hero of Shakespeare's play, and Duncan, the king Macbeth murdered. We are told that near the remains of the Scottish kings are the bones of four Irish kings, and no less than eight kings of Norway.

Much of Iona's reputation for sanctity was derived from the long shadow cast by its first abbot, but it seems that Columba was not content merely to be remembered and prayed for. He also took an active part in human affairs after his death, as when he appeared in a dream dreamed by the aforementioned Oswald, then king of Northumbria, on the eve of the Battle of Heavenfield in 634. On this occasion, Columba delivered another of his prophecies, saying that Oswald would be victorious.

In his book on Iona, Thomas Hannan says that, though some call the island the Rome of Celtic Christianity, he would call it its Jerusalem. One event that has added to Iona's holy reputation was the departure from the island of Saint Aidan, in 635, nearly forty years after the death of Columba.

By this time Oswald had secured his position as king of Northumbria, after winning the aforementioned battle of Heavenfield, near Hexham in the modern county of Northumberland. He replaced

Eanfrith and Osric, two short-lived pagan kings: Eanfrith had ruled Bernicia, the northern part of Northumbria, and Osric Deira, the southern part.

In his *Ecclesiastical History*, Bede tells us that this period, with its pagan kings, was so terrible that, in later years, the Northumbrians wanted to expunge it from history altogether. They duly removed Eanfrith and Osric from their king-lists, and assigned the time during which they reigned to their successor, King Oswald. As a monk, Bede was no doubt keen to pour scorn on this so-called 'hateful year' because it represented the temporary collapse of Christianity in the region.

Both Eanfrith and Osric were killed by Cadwallon, the Christian king of Gwynedd in Wales. Cadwallon seems to have been determined to do as much harm to the Anglo-Saxons who lived to the east of his homeland as possible, and Oswald could not sit securely as king of Northumbria until he had killed the Welshman, and scattered his army. This is what happened at Heavenfield. According to Bede, the place had been known as Heavenfield for a long time before the battle – the founder of English history had no doubt that the ancient naming of the place was a prophecy of the Christian victory that would be obtained there.

Bede tells us that Oswald's force was much smaller than Cadwallon's, but it seems that the lie of the land was against the Welshman. Oswald occupied a strong defensive position, with the Roman Wall at his back (fragments of the Wall still remain at Heavenfield). Before the battle, no doubt inspired by his vision of Columba, Oswald set up an improvised wooden cross, and motivated his troops with a speech in which he invited them to 'kneel, and together beseech the true and living God Almighty in His mercy to defend us from the proud and cruel enemy; for He knows that we have undertaken a just war for the safety of our nation'.

The cross Oswald had erected at Heavenfield was later a focus for veneration, and was responsible for a number of healing miracles. A monk called Bothelm, who lived in the time of Bede – that is to say, a century after the battle – broke his arm after 'walking carelessly on the ice at night'. When he heard that another monk would be travelling to Heavenfield, he begged him to come back with a splinter of Oswald's cross. The monk returned with a piece of the moss that had grown on it, which the injured monk put inside his clothes. He slept all night with the moss tucked away like this, and in the morning he found that he had lost the terrible pain and immobility of the arm that had tormented him since his injury.

Later writers have not failed to compare Oswald's victory at Heavenfield, inspired by a Christian dream, with a victory enjoyed by the Roman Emperor Constantine over three hundred years earlier. This was the Battle of the Milvian Bridge north of Rome, immediately after which Contantine's rival, Maxentius, drowned while fleeing with his army before Constantine's victorious force. Like Oswald, Constantine was visited by an encouraging dream on the eve of the battle. In his dream, he was told that if he painted the Christian symbol of the Chi-Rho on his soldiers' shields, he would win. Constantine later worked to promote Christianity throughout the Roman Empire, though some say that he was not himself baptised until shortly before his death in 337.

Readers who cannot accept that a dead saint could invade the dreams of a sleeping king will no doubt be pleased to hear that Oswald could easily have dreamed of Columba of his own accord, since, as a prince, the king had spent part of a long exile on Iona. Several members of Oswald's family had fled to exile after Edwin became king of Northumbria in 616. Oswald himself probably did not spend the whole period of his exile on Columba's tiny island: he may have travelled to many parts of Dal Riada, and may even have fought in battles in Ireland.

It is likely that wherever he went in Dal Riada, Oswald would have heard stories of Columba, who had died less than ten years before he himself was born. He would no doubt have met people who had known the saint, and visited monasteries founded by Columba and his associates. He became fluent in the Celtic language of the Dal Riadans, which was quite different from his own Germanic mother-tongue, Anglo-Saxon.

Oswald saw his chance to become king of Northumbria when the pagan kings Eanfrith and Osric were killed. Their predecessor, King Edwin of Northumbria, whom Oswald had gone into exile to avoid, had been a Christian, converted by Saint Paulinus of York, one of the missionaries sent from Rome by Gregory the Great.

When Edwin died in battle against Cadwallon and his English ally, the Pagan

King Penda of Mercia, it was as if Paulinus's successful mission to the Northumbrians had never happened. Joseph Lightfoot, a nineteenth-century bishop of Durham, wrote that 'a sponge had passed over Northumbria, and scarce a vestige of his [Paulinus's] work remained'.

The apparent obliteration of Paulinus's legacy of Christianity in Northumbria might have happened because the new faith had had only a few years to 'bed down' among a population whose ancestors had been pagans for thousands of years. As often happened at this time, Paulinus had started his missionary work by trying to convert the royal family and the higher aristocracy. There were many advantages to this approach, but there is evidence to suggest that the degree to which the Word trickled down from the royal court to the ordinary people in their thatched huts may have been limited.

Oswald had been converted to Christianity, and baptised, during his exile in Dal Riada; and when he became king of Northumbria, he set in motion a plan to convert, or re-convert, his subjects to Christianity. Although he was an Anglo-Saxon by ethnicity, King Oswald counts as a Celtic saint because the type of Christianity he had learned in Dal Riada was the Celtic type, and he reached out to Iona and not Rome for help bringing the Word to his people.

At first Segene, the abbot of Iona, sent Oswald a bishop called Corman to convert his people to, or back to, Christianity. (It was a peculiarity of the Celtic system which was followed in Columba's monasteries that abbots could order bishops around, and not vice versa.)

Oswald must have expected great things of Corman, who arrived with a party of fellow-monks to help him with his work. Unfortunately Corman's mission was a complete failure, and he was soon back on Iona again, sitting in on a sort of post-mortem about what had happened.

Corman reported that the people to whom he had been sent as a missionary bishop had not listened to him, because they were intractable, stubborn and barbarous. In response, the future Saint Aidan, who was at the meeting, suggested to Corman that 'you were more severe to your unlearned hearers than you ought to have been, and did not at first, conformably to the Apostolic rule, give them the milk of more easy doctrine, till, being by degrees nourished with the Word of

God, they should be capable of receiving that which is more perfect and of performing the higher precepts of God'.

Aidan's words implied that the process of converting these newcomers to the Word should be handled like the process of weaning a baby off milk and on to solid food. The image is striking, fitting and effective, and very much in line with traditional Christian ideas of religious teaching as a kind of spiritual nourishment. The idea also implies that, with patience, a newcomer's acceptance of the tougher teachings of the church could be as natural as a child's adaptation to solids.

Aidan's speech certainly gained the attention of his brother monks who were present at the meeting, and soon Aidan had been made a bishop, and set off for Oswald's kingdom as Corman's replacement.

The story as told in Bede might give one the idea that Aidan was a humble monk who won the title of bishop through simple insight, and the directness of his speech. The sources state, however, that Aidan was descended from a high king of Ireland, and was even related to St Brigid.

Northumbria, Aidan's destination, was so named because it lay to the north of the

Humber estuary. As an Anglo-Saxon kingdom, its full extent varied, but at times it stretched as far north along the east coast of Great Britain as Edinburgh and the Firth of Forth. The kingdom should not be confused with the modern county of Northumberland, which, as the most northerly English county, does not stretch into Scotland. Northumbria sometimes included what are now the Scottish counties of Lothian and Borders, and the English counties of Northumberland, Durham, and much of Yorkshire.

The first challenge facing Aidan and his companions was the journey of nearly two hundred miles (if they went by land) from Iona, off the west coast of Scotland, east to the North Sea coast. Other challenges included the stubbornness and barbarity that Corman had met with among Oswald's subjects; and the language barrier.

King Oswald made it his personal mission to break through the language barrier for Aidan's benefit. Bede tells us that it was a beautiful sight to see Oswald standing up and translating for Aidan – doing what we would now call a simultaneous translation. Under these circumstances, it would surely have been difficult for Oswald's followers to refuse to listen to the message, as had happened during Corman's failed mission. If they had chatted, gone to sleep or wandered off while their new king was translating, this would surely have been taken as a sign of disloyalty.

Aidan is now eternally associated with one location – the island of Lindisfarne, where he was the first bishop. In Aidan's day, and for a long time afterwards, the island really was an Iona for the newly-converted or re-converted Anglo-Saxon Northumbrians, on the east coast of Great Britain. It acted as the headquarters for the Celtic Christian mission to the Northumbrian people in their northern fastness, and for many years the bishops of Lindisfarne were their spiritual leaders.

While Aidan is associated with Lindisfarne, Oswald is linked with a spectacular location at the edge of the Northumbrian mainland, just a few miles further south along the North Sea coast. This is Bamburgh, where today an impressive stone castle sits on top of a high, flat-topped outcrop of black rock, fronted by a broad beach. The castle on its rock is one of the most impressive of the many fine sights in the North-East, and has often been used as a location for historical costume dramas made for TV and the cinema.

In Oswald's time, the sea would have come right up to the bottom of the east-facing cliff, and this and the steep sides of the rock would have made Bamburgh an easily defensible position. This was important because, as in Ireland and Scotland at this time, there were frequent wars between the petty kings who ruled their own areas of England.

Before the Anglo-Saxons, who were Oswald's ancestors, pushed the Celts into the western parts of Great Britain, Bamburgh had been a Celtic fortress, called Din Guayrdi (perhaps the Dolorous Guard of Arthurian legend). As such it dated right back to pre-Roman times, and the Votadini, the tribe who occupied the place, were known to the Romans in the first century A.D. The modern name 'Bamburgh' may have been derived from the name of Oswald's step-mother, Bebba.

Archaeology suggests that Oswald had a fairly typical royal settlement on top of the rock, complete with a great hall in the Anglo-Saxon style, a church, workshops and dwellings. To reinforce the defences of the site, Bamburgh probably had a heavy wooden rampart around it, from which

Oswald would have been able to look out over the North Sea and the nearby Farne Islands.

The islands, and Bamburgh's rocky crag, are part of the Great Whin Sill, an outcrop of igneous rock that can also be seen at Dunstanburgh Castle, which lies further south along the North Sea coast, and at the High Force waterfall in Teesdale. The Sill also forms the convenient ridge along which parts of Hadrian's Wall were built.

Most fortresses like Bamburgh, naturally defensible sites that have been reinforced by human hands, need to have a good water-supply if they are to hope to resist a siege of any length. There is a very old well that was dug into the hard dolerite rock on which Oswald's fortress stood. This was made by lighting a fire on the rock itself, then dousing the fire with cold water, to make the rock shatter. This painstaking process was then repeated and repeated until water was reached.

In summer, the rock on which Bamburgh Castle stands is very green, thanks to the many hardy plants that have gained a purchase on its steep sides. It is likely that in Anglo-Saxon times the rocks would have been kept free of any vegetation, which could have been used by invaders to climb up to the fortress. Something similar was done later, at Durham, where it was illegal to let trees grow on the sides of the rock on which the castle and cathedral stand, for fear that Scottish invaders would use them as cover.

After Oswald's death an alarming attempt was made to breach the defences of Bamburgh, by the aforementioned Penda, the pagan king of Mercia. At its height, Penda's Anglo-Saxon kingdom of Mercia took up a huge area of central England south of the Humber Estuary – north of that, Northumbria began.

Penda attempted to take Oswald's fortress by fire. This he did by dismantling the nearby village (which would have consisted almost entirely of wooden buildings), piling its ruins up against the rock on one side, then setting it alight.

Given that Oswald's castle would not have been equipped with fire-hoses, anyone present at the time could have seen that only heavy rain, or a change of wind-direction, could save Bamburgh. Luckily Saint Aidan saw the fire from his own spiritual fortress on Lindisfarne, and prayed to God for help. The wind changed straight away, and the fortress was saved.

Although Oswald and the bishop he had 'ordered' from Iona could see each other's homes in the distance, the fact that Aidan had wisely chosen, and been granted, Lindisfarne as his headquarters meant that the two men didn't have to live in each other's pockets.

The island of Lindisfarne is similar in size to Iona, and at high tide a stretch of sea separates it from the mainland, which is similar in breadth to the stretch that separates Iona from the Isle of Mull.

Lindisfarne is not strictly speaking a 'full' island. It is what geographers call a 'tombola', a semi-island that is linked to the mainland at low tide. Today the land that is revealed at low tide consists of sodden mud-flats, with the ancient pilgrim path to Lindisfarne marked out with stakes. Pilgrims who would prefer to keep their feet dry can now cross to the island via a raised causeway.

The priory that visitors see on Lindisfarne today is not Aidan's monastery, although the stone ruins are the remains of later structures that were probably built on the same site. Aidan's buildings would have been much smaller and humbler, built of wood, thatch and wattle-and-daub after the

Anglo-Saxon fashion.

There is no reliable record of the Rule Aidan's monks followed, though it was probably close to the Columban Rule as it existed on Iona; and hints of this have been preserved in Adomnan's Life of Columba, and in other records.

In the sources, the monks are often referred to as 'soldiers of Christ', and as such they were prepared to undertake long, perilous journeys and strenuous physical work in Jesus' name. The brothers owned everything in common, and were not supposed to regard anything as a personal possession. In the same spirit, they gave charity to the needy, and were hospitable to strangers and other visitors: some visitors were allowed to stay in the monastery, or nearby, indefinitely.

The brethren took a vow of celibacy, and this rule was strictly enforced. Once they were accepted as monks, they received the Celtic tonsure, which was different from the Roman Catholic version, but still marked the monk as somebody who was different from non-monks.

The Celtic tonsure later became one of the bones of contention between the Roman and the Celtic churches. Whereas the

Romans had their heads shaved so that their remaining hair formed a ring or crown around a central shaven area, the Celts shaved the front of the head, and let the hair at the back grow freely.

Study and education were important elements of what went on in the monasteries, and it will be remembered that, even as he felt his death approaching, Columba asked a fellow-monk to complete the copy of the psalms that he, Columba, had been making.

In his book on Aidan, A.C. Fryer paints an attractive picture of the monastic school on Lindisfarne. Here the young students would sit in their school-room, with their waxed tablets, on which they could scratch out letters, then later erase them by smoothing out the wax. Since all books at this time were rare, precious, hand-made and hand-written, they were hung up on the walls in leather satchels, so as to be protected from rats and, with luck, from damp.

Among the students of this school who later went on to great things were St Chad, St Cedd and St Wilfrid. Despite his early education at Lindisfarne, the headquarters of Celtic Christianity in Northumbria, Wilfrid, who later became an abbot and a bishop, turned against the Celtic Church; as we shall see.

As well as producing their own books, the monastic communities were pretty self-contained in terms of many of their other needs as well: they even made their own plain garments, from the wool of their own sheep.

The monks' habits consisted of a white under-garment, with a coarse woollen hood and robe worn over it. The wool was allowed to retain its natural colour, so that the brothers would have had a rather oatmealy appearance. They slept in these clothes, so bed-clothes were not needed. For trips outside in cold weather, they would have worn a cloak for extra protection.

They grew their own grain and vegetables, raised their own farm-animals, and baked their own bread. The resulting diet was very plain, and the monks would have tasted meat very rarely: mainly during festivals, or when there was an important guest. During Lent, strict fasting was the rule.

For pious, studious monks, brothers who liked peace and quiet, men unsuited to family life or life as a warrior, and those who felt inspired by the presence of Aidan as their bishop, the life of the monastery must have seemed idyllic. Here they had access to one of the best educations available in Europe at the time, and they could read, and take part in the creation of, those precious and all-important books.

The monastic life was so attractive to some people that they embraced it despite high social status in the secular world, abandoning lives of comparative luxury and influence. Saint Cuthbert, who later filled Aidan's role as bishop of Lindisfarne, almost certainly came from a privileged aristocratic background, as did Hilda of Whitby. King Sigeberht of the East Angles even abdicated so that he could take up the monastic life.

At times, though, the life of the brothers must have seemed narrow, repetitive and harsh. Sometimes the monks embraced an even greater degree of asceticism, or deliberate hard living, by, for instance, immersing themselves in cold water while reciting psalms.

When King Oswald visited Bishop Aidan and his monks, he would have partaken of their simple food. By contrast, when Aidan visited Oswald's court, he would presumably have been offered rather richer fare, and would have had the opportunity to enjoy a royal blow-out, get royally drunk and then sleep the whole thing off in some luxurious apartment in the palace. Bede tells us that Aidan did not take up this opportunity: instead he came to Oswald's feasts attended by a few of his monks, and they left early, having eaten very little, before things got too riotous.

On one famous Easter Sunday Aidan was about to break bread with Oswald when they heard about a number of poor people waiting outside, begging for food. The king immediately ordered that his own meal should be sent out to them, together with the silver dish it had been served on: the dish was to be divided equally among the beggars.

Impressed by Oswald's charity, Aidan blessed the royal hand that had made this charitable gesture. 'May this hand never perish,' he said. Given the fate that Oswald met only a few years after he had gained his kingdom of Northumbria, Aidan's blessing is often interpreted as a prediction that, after his death, the royal hand would remain 'incorrupt', impervious to decay, like the whole bodies of many other saints.

Although Bede says he ruled wisely, re-united Northumbria, and attempted to spread brotherly love by promoting the Christian religion, Oswald still had enemies left over from the wars that had put him on his throne.

Cadwallon, the king of Gwynedd, had died in battle against Oswald, but Penda, his pagan partner in crime, had survived. He soon brought a mixed army of Mercians and Welshmen against the Northumbrian king.

Oswald's last battle was at a place called Maserfeth, which is usually identified as Oswestry in Shropshire. The Welsh historian Nennius suggested that Penda used black arts to help him win the battle and kill Oswald. However he did it, Oswald lay dead at the end of the day, and his head and arms were placed on poles, perhaps as an offering to the god Woden. A year later, Oswald's successor, his brother Oswiu, came to collect the remains. He found that one of the arms was in a miraculous state of preservation.

Although Aidan continued to be bishop over the whole of Northumbria, the kingdom split into its two constituent parts again after Oswald's death. The late king's brother Oswiu ruled Bernicia, the northern part, while Deira, the southern part, was taken by Oswin, a representative of the family of King Edwin, who had been converted to Christianity by Paulinus.

The two Northumbrian kingdoms were soon at war with each other. Realising that defeat at the hands of his rival Oswiu was inevitable, Oswin disbanded his own army and fled to the house of a nobleman called Hunwold. There he was assassinated.

Oswin's death had been prophesied by Aidan. The Deiran king had given Aidan the gift of a fine horse with royal trappings, but in a gesture reminiscent of St Brigid of Ireland, the saint gave away the horse and all its glittering accoutrements to a poor beggar.

Oswin remonstrated with Aidan, then realised how un-Christian he had been to resent the saint's actions, and threw himself at Aidan's feet. At this, the saint was struck with the thought that such a good king could surely not live long, and began to weep.

Aidan himself lasted only twelve days after Oswin was killed. The seventeenth-century Durham writer Robert Hegge observed that the saint thought it was a sin to live long after such a good king had died. Aidan expired leaning against a wooden buttress on the outside of a church on one of the royal estates. After his death, the church was burned down during a raid by Penda's forces, but the buttress miraculously untouched by the flames. When the rebuilt church was burned down again, this time by accident, Aidan's buttress was still unburned.

It is said that a young man who was working as a shepherd nearby saw Aidan's soul being carried up 'into the heavenly country' by angels, amid much streaming light, on the night that he died. The young man, who later became St Cuthbert, was moved by this experience to travel to the monastery at Old Melrose on the River Tweed to become a monk. Cuthbert, who spent the first part of his career as a Celtic Christian, changed lanes into the Roman stream of Christianity when Oswiu, the King of Northumbria, opted for the Roman approach.

After the death of his rival Oswin, Oswiu's power was still limited by the continued existence of Penda of Mercia. When Penda was finally killed at the Battle of the Winwaed in 655, Oswiu's sway over Great Britain began to approach the degree of power that had been enjoyed by his brother Oswald.

Perhaps in an attempt to unite his own family with the rival Northumbrian dynasty, from which King Edwin had sprung, Oswiu, who had been raised as a Celtic Christian, took Eanfled, Edwin's daughter, as his second wife. Like her father, who had been converted by Paulinus, Eanfled followed the Roman form of Christianity.

V. Twilight of the Celtic Saints

When he has given his account of the death of Aidan, whom he clearly regarded as a great man, Bede takes a minute to write about the saint's faults as a Christian. From Bede's point of view, these were all to do with his provenance as a Celtic Christian.

Bede wrote two books on time, and was an expert on the complex business of how Christians calculate the date of Easter. The fact that, in some years, Celtic Christians celebrated Easter on a different day to the one marked by Roman Christians meant that Bede could not accept Aidan and his followers as fully Christian. For Bede, the Celtic tonsure and way of calculating Easter were powerful symbols of a degree of inadequacy in the version of Christianity that the Celtic missionary saints had brought with them from Ireland. By implication, Bede also seems to be telling his readers that a Church that celebrates Easter on the right day has more legitimacy.

Unlike Christmas Day, which always falls on the twenty-fifth of December, Easter Sunday, as celebrated by Christians who use the modern Roman or Gregorian system, can happen on a Sunday between the twenty-second of March and the twenty-fifth of April. For Eastern Orthodox Christians, Easter Day can fall on a different Sunday: in 2016, Gregorian Easter was Sunday March the twenty-seventh, whereas for Orthodox Christians who follow the Julian calendar, Easter Sunday fell on May the first. (According to the Gregorian system, Easter Day cannot happen in May at all).

The resurrection of Jesus, which is supposed to have happened at the time of the Jewish Passover festival, is the central event in the Christian narrative, and it is that that is commemorated on Easter Sunday. The Jews celebrate Passover on the first full moon after the spring equinox, but to calculate the date of Easter, the Christians of Bede's time did not merely find out when any local Jews were celebrating Passover: in fact some methods for calculating the date were rejected because they seemed to be too similar to the Jewish approach to calculating the date of Passover.

The Jews had a lunar calendar, whereas

the Christians had a solar calendar. Part of the trick of calculating Easter was therefore to find a way for these lunar and solar calendars to work together. The Christians also insist on celebrating Easter Day on a Sunday, whereas for the Jews, Passover can happen on any day of the week.

One answer to the problem was to devise a calendar which lasted for several years, which could then be used again and again throughout the centuries. Bede favoured a nineteen-year calendar. Nineteen was a significant number for Bede, because he had described a system for counting to nineteen using the joints and tips of the fingers of one hand. The nineteen-year system was not invented by Bede, but was first used by a third-century Syrian bishop called Anatolius of Laodicea.

As described by Bede, Aidan's way of calculating Easter was simply to plump for the Sunday that fell between the fourteenth and twentieth days of the new moon (coincidentally, in 2016 'Aidan's Easter Sunday' would have been the twenty-seventh of March: exactly the same as the Roman Catholic one). Bede implies that this method was crude compared to his preferred technique; but in his *Ecclesiastical History* the father of English history seems to be scandalised by the idea that anyone would think that Aidan celebrated Easter on any day of the week other than a Sunday.

Although it is unlikely that many modern Christians are as offended by the non-Roman way of calculating Easter as Bede was, the issue, known as the paschal controversy, is still a live one in the twenty-first century. The Catholic pope Francis has recently indicated a willingness to discuss a new unified approach to the problem, as has Justin Welby, the present Archbishop of Canterbury, and the Coptic pope Tawadros II.

Bede tells us that, in some years, the Celtic and Roman Easters were so far apart in the calendar that King Oswiu sometimes found himself feasting on Easter Sunday when his wife, Eanfled, was still observing Lent.

Clearly, there was no way that the inconvenience suffered by an English king could cause the Celtic and Roman churches to unify, thus ending the paschal controversy, in Britain at least. No doubt influenced by discussions with Queen Eanfled and her Roman-Christian followers, Oswiu proposed a meeting at which he hoped to see the whole business thrashed out.

This was the famous Synod of Whitby, hosted by Hilda, the abbess of Whitby and one of the last English Celtic saints.

Whitby lies at the mouth of the river Esk, near the North Sea coast of Yorkshire, some forty miles north-east of York itself. A small town, it punches well above its weight in terms of history, good looks and attractiveness for tourists. A Celtic-style stone cross erected in a church-yard above the town commemorates not only Hilda but her contemporary, Caedmon, said to be the first English poet. Bede tells us that Caedmon was a lay servant of Hilda's abbey who fell asleep in the cow-shed one night. He woke up with his head full of beautiful spiritual songs in the English language of his time – the language we now call Anglo-Saxon, or Old English.

Local jet – a hard black stone that can be carved to make shiny jewellery and ornaments – is a famous product of Whitby, as well as another geological rarity – the large numbers of fossils that can be found there. The town was also a whaling port, and an arch formed of whale-bone still stands there as a monument to this industry.

The picturesque qualities of the place

have long been recognised – the Victorian photographer Frank Meadow Sutcliffe took many fine pictures of the town and its people. Whitby is also an important setting in the novel *Dracula* by Bram Stoker, published in 1897.

There is a link between the town's famous fossils and Saint Hilda, the abbess and hostess of the 664 synod of Whitby. The town's coat of arms features three ammonites which look more like coiled-up snakes than ammonites proper. This is a reference to the story that relates that Hilda changed all the local snakes into stones – a pious explanation of the appearance of these fossils from a time long before their true nature was understood.

At the synod of Whitby, the Celtic tonsure was discussed, but Bede's account focuses on the arguments over the vexed question of the calculation of the date of Easter.

While King Oswui sat back and watched, the two sides slugged it out. In the Celtic corner were Bishop Colman of Lindisfarne, Abbess Hilda, and Cedd, Bishop of the East Saxons, among others. The champion for the Roman side was the aforementioned Wilfrid, educated at Aidan's (Celtic) monastery on Lindisfarne, but a convert to the Roman cause.

Since leaving Lindisfarne, Wilfrid had gained the patronage of several Anglo-Saxon royals, and travelled to Kent, France and Rome. In the Eternal City the well-travelled Northumbrian had acquired a knowledge of, and admiration for, the Roman way of doing things, including the calculation of Easter, and the power-structure of the continental church. He had also built up a portable collection of holy relics.

On his return to England, Alchfrith, King Oswiu's son, had made Wilfrid master of the monastery at Ripon. Wilfrid was not happy with the monks there, however, though they included among their number the young St Cuthbert, and he replaced them with a new abbot and monks, who were more to his taste.

His summary dismissal of the original Ripon monks was entirely typical of Wilfrid's high-handed approach to his role in the church: he was liable to find fault everywhere, especially among his fellow Englishmen. He was like one of those people who always think that anything foreign must be better. Such people are satirised by Laurence Sterne in his 1768 book *A Sentimental Journey Through France and*

Italy.

Sterne's book opens with the sentence 'They order, said I, this matter better in France,' and, at least when it came to matters concerning the church, Wilfrid would certainly have agreed. When it came to his ordination, his high-handedness compelled him to insist that he be ordained by Agilbert, a French bishop then living in England. This Agilbert was present in Wilfrid's corner at the Synod of Whitby.

Although he was only in his mid-thirties when he participated in the fateful synod, Wilfrid's arguments, as presented by Bede in his *Ecclesiastical History*, won the day, convinced King Oswiu, and put the unfortunate Colman, bishop of Lindisfarne, in an isolated and untenable position.

Colman argued that the method he used to calculate the date of Easter was the one used by John, the 'beloved disciple' of Jesus. Wilfrid insisted that this could not be the case, because John did not care on what day of the week Easter fell, whereas the Christians of later times knew that it had to happen on a Sunday.

Wilfrid, who did not hesitate to call the Celtic Christians 'stupid' for their adherence to what he saw as the wrong way of calculating Easter, also claimed that his way was the one practised in Rome, France, Africa, Asia, Greece and Egypt. According to the young abbot, only the Picts and the Britons persisted in following the wrong method. Part of Wilfrid's statement may seem a little strange to modern readers, because even today the Greek Orthodox Church and the Coptic Christians of Egypt do not always celebrate Easter at the same time as the Roman Catholics.

The champion of the Roman way then went on to describe how St Peter himself, the disciple of Jesus and first bishop of Rome, calculated Easter, according to Wilfrid's approved method.

Colman countered by claiming that the method he used was that of Anatolius of Laodicea, the aforementioned Syrian bishop who had introduced the cycle of nineteen years as an aid to calculating Easter. Colman coupled this argument with an assertion of the saintly status of Columba and his successors: how could these men, whose holiness was confirmed by so many miracles, have been wrong?

Wilfrid responded to Colman's point about Anatolius by explaining in detail why Colman and his monks were not following

Anatolius's system at all, because, according to Wilfrid, they did not even understand when a particular day can be said to have started.

Tackling Colman's assertion that great Christians like Columba could not have been mistaken in their approach to Easter, the hot-headed Wilfrid nearly went too far. He alluded to a passage in the gospel of Matthew, part of the Sermon on the Mount (Chapter 7, verses 21-3). Here Jesus tells us that:

Not every one that saith unto me, Lord, Lord, shall enter into the kingdom of heaven; but he that doeth the will of my Father which is in heaven. Many will say to me in that day, Lord, Lord, have we not prophesied in thy name? and in thy name have cast out devils? and in thy name done many wonderful works? And then will I profess unto them, I never knew you: depart from me, ye that work iniquity.

(KJV)

In the context of the passage, Jesus may be referring to the 'evil fruit' and corrupt trees he mentions slightly earlier; and also to the 'false prophets, who come to you in sheep's clothing, but inwardly they are ravening wolves'.

Wilfrid's allusion to this gospel passage must have raised the hairs on the backs of the necks of some of the attenders at the Synod of Whitby. There may have been a sudden silence, broken only by embarrassed coughing and sharp intakes of breath. Looking around and perhaps spotting some red faces, and some very pale ones, Wilfrid started to back-pedal.

He claimed that he did not say this in reference to Columba and his successors: after all, it was much better to think well of people one had never met. And of course those saints of days gone by did not know any better: they had not yet been told the correct way to calculate Easter.

Wilfrid wound up his arguments by asserting that Columba was in effect outranked by St Peter, chief of the apostles, to whom Jesus had given the very keys of heaven. Concluding the discussion, King Oswiu expressed his concern that if Peter held the keys, then Northumbria should follow his way of doing things. The king did not want to reach the gates of heaven after his death, only to find that St Peter turned his back on him.

Bede tells us that everyone at the synod

agreed with the king, but the historian then goes on to describe how Colman, unable to give up the old ways, resigned his bishopric of Lindisfarne and returned to Ireland, with a party of English and Irish monks who were prepared to remain loyal to the Celtic way.

And so another island enters our story: the island of Inisbofin, or 'the Island of the White Cow,' off the Atlantic coast of Ireland, where Colman founded a new monastery along Celtic Christian lines. But Colman had not left Northumbria empty-handed. He took a fragment of the True Cross with him, and some of the bones of St Aidan.

VI. Reflections

In his book *The Rise of Western Christendom*, Peter Brown describes Wilfrid's victory as a push against an open door. Christians in many parts of the British Isles had already adopted the Roman Easter, and more and more monks were sporting the Roman tonsure. The dispute held at Hilda's abbey had of course been to do with more than just a calendar and a haircut, however. If that had been all that was on the table, Celtic Christianity would not have survived as an issue of intense interest to many modern Christians.

The type of Christianity that suffered such a blow at Whitby might have remained a forgotten dead-end in British ecclesiastical history, if enthusiasts in the eighteenth, nineteenth and twentieth centuries had not brought Celtic Christianity, and Celtic culture in general, back out into the light. Some modern devotees claim that the Celtic

Christianity of Patrick, Brigid, Columba and Aidan was different from, and perhaps preferable to, other types of Christianity that were extant in the early middle ages, or existed earlier, or have appeared since.

The tales of the Celtic saints related above do have things in common that make them distinctive, but it should not be supposed that these similarities are necessarily distinctively Celtic.

The stories of Patrick and Brigid in particular have a lot of pastoral elements: they generally seem to take place in the open air, in the Irish countryside. Cows, milk and even butter feature prominently, and St Patrick is often riding about in his chariot when things happen. Both Brigid and Patrick have to deal with the Irish weather, but all this does not necessarily make their Celtic Christian stories closer to nature than other stories from the same period, or earlier, or even much later.

In the middle ages, European populations were predominantly rural. Overall, the numbers of people were very small by modern standards; European cities and towns were comparatively small, and the rural work of feeding the population was very labour-intensive. Because light and heat were wasteful and problematic inside a building, people spent a lot of time outside, especially during summer days, when there was enough natural light and heat to allow them to live their lives outside in relative comfort.

Whereas today, speedy means of travel such as cars, planes and trains take us away from nature, which can become little more than a moving picture scrolling past the window, travel in the early medieval period put travellers into a closer relationship with the realities of wild nature than many would have liked. None of these differences between our modern world and the greener universe of the Celtic Christians are unique to Celtic Christianity.

It has been said that Celtic Christianity lived closer to its pagan roots than other forms of the Christian faith; but examples from all over the Christian world show that a degree of intermingling of pagan and Christian cultural elements was commonplace. In English, the Christian spring festival is named after a pagan festival or goddess: Eostre. Likewise Christmas is related to the Roman festival of the Saturnalia, and many would say that many more Christian saints than just Brigid share characteristics with heathen gods. The most striking example of this is the Virgin Mary, who is similar in many respects to the ancient Roman goddess Diana: a virgin goddess associated with the moon.

Some aspects of Celtic Christianity that have been singled out as particularly Celtic in character can be traced back to older Christian traditions that originated well outside the Celtic sphere of influence. The extreme level of asceticism, or deliberate hard living, of the Celtic monks and saints was something that is said to have distinguished them from the Roman saints, but then Gregory, who sent Roman missionaries to England in the first place, lived very plainly. Many regard the originator of ascetic monasticism as St Antony of Egypt, who was hardly a Celt. A Christian ascetic whose example literally stood above all others was Simeon Stylites ('Simeon the Stylite'), who lived on a narrow platform on top of a pillar in Syria for thirty-seven years. As well as happening outside the Celtic Christian tradition, this sort of thing can also be seen today outside Christianity altogether. The Hindu sadhus and aghoris of India will refuse to wash (like St Antony), make themselves dirty by rolling along the ground instead of walking, sleep on beds of cactuses, and perform such feats as keeping one arm up in the air, or standing on one leg, for long periods.

An Irish saint-story that combines extreme ascetic behaviour with kindness and love of nature, but also reminds us of the feats of the Hindu sadhus, is a tale told of St Kevin. Kevin, who is associated with County Wicklow, kept his body still for a very long time during what must have been a sort of marathon of prayer and meditation. He stayed so still that a blackbird built a nest in his hand and laid her eggs. The saint continued to be immobile long enough for the eggs to hatch and the chicks to grow old enough to fly away.

In her 1971 book on the Celts, Nora Chadwick identified a certain linguistic ingenuity, and a love of eloquence, as a particular quality of Celtic culture; and certainly there is a vividness and directness, combined with a down-to-earth quality, in key Celtic texts, which is very attractive. This is not, however, unique to the Celts, who remained open to influences from a diverse range of cultures even before they embraced Christianity. The aforementioned *Patrick's Breastplate*, also known as *Patrick's Lorica* or *The Cry of the Deer*, is an oft-quoted poem in which the saint describes himself as putting on spiritual armour, including the Trinity, the baptism of Christ, the love of the angels, etc. This is taken by some to be a defining text of the Celtic Christian faith, yet in the New Testament Letter to the Ephesians we find a very similar idea:

Put on the whole armour of God, that ye may be able to stand against the wiles of the devil . . . Wherefore take unto you the whole armour of God, that ye may be able to withstand in the evil day, and having done all, to stand. Stand therefore, having your loins girt about with truth, and having on the breastplate of righteousness; And your feet shod with the preparation of the gospel of peace; Above all, taking the shield of faith, wherewith ye shall be able to quench all the fiery darts of the wicked. And take the helmet of salvation, and the sword of the Spirit, which is the word of God . . .

(Ephesians 6, 11, 13-17, KJV)

Select Bibliography

Adomnan of Iona: *Life of St Columba* (trans. Richard Sharpe), Penguin, 1991

Bartlett, Robert: *Why Can the Dead Do Such Great Things?*, Princeton, 2013

Bede: *The Ecclesiastical History of the English People* (trans. Judith McClure and Roger Collins), Oxford, 1999

Bede: *Bede's Ecclesiastical History of England* (trans. A.M. Sellar), George Bell, 1907

Bradley, Ian: *Columba: Pilgrim and Penitent*, 597-1997, Wild Goose, 1996

Brooks, J.A.: *Mull, Iona & Staffa*, Jarrold, 1998

Brown, Peter: *The Rise of Western Christendom: Triumph and Diversity, A.D.*

200-1000, Wiley, 2013

Chadwick, Nora: *The Celts*, Penguin, 1997

Culling, Elizabeth: *What is Celtic Christianity?*, Grove, 1994

Davies, Oliver (trans.): *Celtic Spirituality*, Paulist, 1999

Duncan, Anthony: *The Elements of Celtic Christianity*, Element, 1992

Dzon, Mary: *The Quest for the Christ-Child in the Later Middle Ages*, University of Pennsylvania Press, 2017

Forbes, A.P.: *Kalendars of Scottish Saints*, Edmonston and Douglas, 1872

Foster, Sally M.: *Picts, Gaels and Scots: Early Historic Scotland*, Birlinn, 2014

Fryer, Alfred C.: *Aidan: The Apostle of England*, S.W. Partridge, 1902

Guirand, Felix (ed.) *New Larousse Encyclopedia of Mythology*, Hamlyn, 1968

Hannan, Thomas: *Iona: And Some Satellites*,

Chambers, 1926

Hanson, R.P.C.: *Saint Patrick: His Origins and Career*, Oxford, 1968

Hull, Eleanor: *Pagan Ireland*, M.H. Gill, 1908

Lightfoot, Joseph: *Leaders in the Northern Church*, Macmillan, 1892

Macalister, R.A.S: *Tara: A Pagan Sanctuary of Ancient Ireland*, Scribner's, 1931

Nennius: *Historia Brittonum*, from *Six Old English Chronicles*, ed. J.A. Giles, Bohn, 1848

O'Donnell, Manus: *Betha Colaim Chille: Life of Columcille*, University of Illinois, 1918

Olden, Thomas (trans.): *The Confession of St. Patrick*, James McGlashan, 1853

Parbury, Kathleen: *The Saints of Lindisfarne*, Frank Graham, 1970

Pochin Mould, D.D.C: *Ireland of the Saints*, Batsford, 1953

Reeves, William (ed.): *The life of St Columba founder of Hy, written by Adamnan*, Dublin University Press, 1857

Rolleston, T.W.: *Myths and Legends of the Celtic Race*, Constable, 1911

Sterne, Laurence: *A Sentimental Journey and Other Writings*, Oxford, 2008

Tristram, Kate: *The Story of Holy Island: An Illustrated History*, Canterbury, 2009

Webb, D.F. and Farmer, D.H. (eds.): *The Age of Bede*, Penguin, 1998

For free downloads and more from the Langley Press, visit our website: http://tinyurl.com/lpdirect

Printed in Great Britain
by Amazon